GET IT FIXI

GET IT FIXED IN IRELAND

Marion FitzGerald

APPLETREE PRESS

Published and printed by
The Appletree Press Ltd
7 James Street South
Belfast BT2 8DL
1992

British Library Cataloguing-in-Publication Data
A catalogue record for this book is
available from the British Library.

ISBN 0 86281 303 4

9 8 7 6 5 4 3 2 1

preface

For almost fourteen years I wrote a column called 'Home Matters' for *The Irish Times*. During these years I came across many interesting people who provided useful and necessary services of one kind or another. I also collected a substantial amount of practical advice from a variety of people working in many different fields – people who were kind enough to share their knowledge and experience with me. I suppose you could call this book a distillation of this information.

There are some points I feel I must make. The electrical and domestic appliance is the product of a very volatile business, and volatile is putting it kindly. Agencies change, distributors change, retailers come and go; and even in the course of writing this book I came across quite a number of modifications in the process of happening, so to speak. So while I have done my very best to check and double check, and check again, it is possible that by the time this book is published other changes may have occurred.

There are some golden rules about domestic appliances. If you have bought one, and it breaks down, **the first people to contact are the people from whom you bought it**, and this is obviously essential if the appliance is still under guarantee. If the appliance is out of guarantee, the cost of repairs will not be covered, but the retailer should be able to have it repaired for a charge, or be able to tell you who you should call to have it fixed.

If, for some reason, you cannot contact a dealer who handles the appliance, or if you had the appliance for some time and don't know who does the servicing, then hopefully you will find a helpful name and address in this book. I have not given the name of every person North and South who services a particular appliance. This was not practical, as the book would have run to three times its present length. What I have given is a contact name or the name of the main dealer or service agent who will organise repairs for you, or tell you where to go in your immediate area.

Telephone numbers are being changed on a regular basis as telephone services are improved and upgraded. Many six-digit Dublin numbers have become seven-digit numbers in the spring 1992 Dublin telephone directory. I have given the new numbers. In other parts of the country, numbers will change later on in the year; in these cases I have given the number as it is at the time of going to press and as it will remain for some months afterwards. If you have any trouble with a number, check the new directory when it comes out for a particular area.

I would not like to claim that this book is exhaustive and that it covers every possible contingency, or lists every useful service. It doesn't. It is a personal list – but I hope people will find it helpful and worthwhile. There are, as well, undoubtedly many people in Dublin and around the country who provide services of whose existence I am unaware, and I would like to hear from them. Hopefully they will write to me and tell me what they do, and perhaps if this book proves successful, I will be able to include them in a future edition.

telephone numbers

The telephone systems in both the Republic of Ireland and Northern Ireland are fully automatic for both national and international calls. In this book, area codes need only be dialled when phoning a number outside your own area.

To call a Northern Ireland number from the Republic of Ireland, dial **08** followed by the area code and number (**084** followed by the number only if it's within the Belfast area).

To call a Republic of Ireland number from Northern Ireland, replace the area code below with the number in the right-hand column.

Town	Area Code	Dial
Buncrana	(077)	0003
Bundoran	(072)	0017
Cavan	(049)	0014
Cork	(021)	0002
Drogheda	(041)	0011
Dublin	(01)	010 353 1
Dundalk	(042)	0004
Galway	(091)	0009
Limerick	(061)	0006
Monaghan	(047)	0013
Sligo	(071)	0015
Waterford	(051)	0005

Republic of Ireland numbers may also be obtained from Northern Ireland by inserting **10353** between the first digit (zero) and the remaining digits of the area code. For example, to phone a Killarney number, area code (064), first dial 010 353 64 and then the number.

To reach Dublin from Northern Ireland, there is no longer a shortcut. Dial **010 353 1** and then the number.

acronyms

IPCRA means that the person listed is a member of the Irish Professional Conservators and Restorers Association.

• aeg

Spare Parts Centre
9 North Frederick Street
Dublin 1
☎ Dublin 726565
(*Republic of Ireland*)

G. & O. Services
Kilwee Industrial Estate
Upper Dunmurry Lane
Belfast BT17 OHD
☎ 0232 301121
(*Northern Ireland*)

• aluminium window and door repairs

Simarc Engineering Co. Ltd
4a Kilbarrack Industrial Estate
Sutton
Dublin 5
☎ Dublin 393679

• amana refrigeration

F. E. Smith Electrical Ltd
3/5 Camden Place
Dublin 2
☎ Dublin 751702

• amstrad

Computers:

DDT Maintenance (Ireland) Ltd
Unit 3, Sandyford Park
Sandyford Industrial Estate
Dublin 18
☎ Dublin 2954888

TVs, radios and satellite receivers:

FMS Video and TV
3 Arran Quay
Dublin
☎ Dublin 710055

For the names of service dealers in Northern Ireland, contact Amstrad PLC.

Amstrad PLC
Brentwood House
169 King's Road
Brentwood
Essex CM14 4EF
☎ 0302 772 28888

• anim name tapes

Catherine Sargent
PO Box 1641
Dublin 13
☎ Dublin 846221l

antiques

There are antique shops all over Ireland, and antique shops can be very tempting places. Undoubtedly, there are still bargains to be had; but how do you go about finding a bargain? Are you likely to find one in an antique dealer's shop?

'A bargain is a relative term', I was once told by a leading antique dealer in Dublin. 'You can buy something well worth the money in a dealer's shop if you know what you're looking at. Nobody is going to *tell* you it's a bargain. You must know what you are about, and there are some people who wouldn't know a bargain if it hit them on the head.'

Prices will vary. 'If you are at one level of antique dealing, you will ask one price; but the fellow who is a bigger dealer or a more important dealer or in a different locality will ask for more money', said my antique dealer friend. 'It will be the same article, but it will be handled at a different level of price. So it all depends on what you're looking for and what your knowledge is. You could come into my shop and I might sell you a thing for £5,000; you could go into Partridges in Bond Street in London and be asked £50,000 for the same thing. It could still be worth the money – it's a very relative term what a bargain is.

'If you go round the provincial antique trade you should, in theory, be able to buy for less than you would in the Dublin trade. The Dublin dealer's expenses are heavier, his stocks are probably greater. Many things go into the making of the price of an antique. You have to discuss prices with dealers. Yes, of course you can beat them down. I wanted to call my newest shop ONO – "or near offer" – but my wife wouldn't let me. I can truthfully say, in fifty years of dealing I have never, ever got the price I asked for.'

Which is the most likely area of antiques to explore? 'You should go for the first twenty or thirty years of the nineteenth century in Irish furniture. Buy nothing unless it is of good quality. Look at the way it's made. Rubbishy drawer linings should be a warning – if the drawer linings are bad, the piece is usually bad. You want things in reasonable condition, because the cost of doing them up is astronomical, and not every cabinet maker is qualified to restore them. Look for good colour. You want things in good condition, of good quality and of good colour.

Irish silver is always worth an investment. Eighteenth-century Irish silver – ordinary domestic things like tea services and cutlery – are well worth buying. Any good porcelain made between 1770 and 1850 is always of interest – again, condition is important.'

Antique shops:

Anybody interested in antiques will have their own favourite antique shop. My favourite is **Ann McCarthy's** little shop in Paul's Lane, Cork city, just a few yards away from Patrick's Street and Patrick's Bridge. This is not the kind of antique shop where the bell rings gently, voices are hushed, and you're afraid to move because you might knock against some precious object. The chances are that you *will* knock against something in Anne's shop, because, if Anne will forgive me, it is a shop of the most glorious clutter – interesting clutter, unusual clutter, fascinating clutter, but definitely clutter. Yet nothing seems to get broken, perhaps because the more breakable objects are out of knocking reach.

I like Anne's shop because it is an antique shop in which most people can afford to buy. You can buy a small Victorian silver spoon from £7, individual old glasses from about £5, an old silver thimble from £20. There are more expensive pieces as well, such as a vinaigrette box in gold and silver for £200, or pieces of old Cork silver, which is highly prized nowadays – an ordinary teaspoon in old Cork silver would cost you about £35, a serving spoon would cost you £200 or more.

There is old lace and old linen. There are silver-backed brush-and-comb sets which once graced dressing-tables; there is old china, bundles of little dessert knives and forks, elegant silver ladles, old clocks, and Victorian table centrepieces. This is a shop in which it is a pleasure to rummage, and clearly many people enjoy the pleasure because the shop almost always seems to be full.

The shop is also special because of Anne herself and because of the interest she takes and the service she gives. Not only does she sell antiques, she knows a great deal about what she stocks. 'People', she says, 'like a little history with what they buy. They want to know where it came from and exactly what it's meant for.' Furthermore, if Anne hasn't got what a customer wants, she'll try to procure it for them. If a customer wants to know who can repair or restore or revive something, the chances are that Anne will know the right tradesperson. People seem to come to see her as much to ask questions as to buy. Not surprisingly, she's been interested in antiques for many years. 'I started by restoring boxes, all kinds of boxes, from writing boxes to jewellery boxes – anything with a lid and hinges on it. I went to a number of courses, but probably learned more working on my own. If you do something yourself over a long period, you can learn a lot; you find out by the process of making mistakes.'

One course from which she *did* learn a lot was a Start Your Own Business course, 'one of the very first. It was held in the Killiney Court Hotel in Dublin, and over a six-month period I travelled up and down from Cork, sometimes for a couple of weeks, sometimes for two or three days at a time.' Anne didn't open the shop until her three children 'were grown up and sorted out'. Her husband Jerry was made redundant about the same time, and together they started the business a few years ago. She particularly likes lace and silver and knows a lot about china and glass, though not much, she says, about paintings or jewellery, 'which is why you don't see paintings or jewellery in the shop, or furniture. You must stick to what you know. The most important aspect of all of this is that we set this business up to have fun, not to be too serious. It's still fun.' It's also fun to visit her shop. You can telephone Anne at ☎ Cork 273755.

• aquatron showers

Ideal Service
Kylemore Park West
Ballyfermot
Dublin 10
☎ Dublin 6266720
(*Republic of Ireland*)

Domestic Sales and Repair Services
219 Kingsway
Dunmurry
Belfast BT17 9SB
☎ 0232 301533
(*Northern Ireland*)

• archaeological artifacts, restored

Dr Christina Haywood
(IPCRA)
19 Maretimo Gardens East
Blackrock
Co. Dublin
☎ Dublin 2833493

architecture

Architects:

You're going to build a house, or add on an extension to an existing house, and you are thinking of employing an architect. How do you choose one? This is something that requires careful consideration. John Graby, general secretary of the Royal Institute of Architects of Ireland, says you should talk to several architects, at least two or three, before you make a decision. 'Ask if you can see work they have done not just recently, but over a number of years. Consider whether you will both get on together and if you can have a reasonable working relationship. Yes, you can use an architect you know, but it should be on a strictly business level, and you might be better off with one who isn't a friend.'

If you don't know of any architects, you can telephone the **Royal Institute of Architects of Ireland**, ☎ Dublin 761703, and they will give you the names of two or three architects in your own area. I think getting an architect who lives near you could be very important. An architect who works nearby is more likely to call and inspect fairly frequently, and also knows that if something goes wrong, he is going to have to meet you on a regular basis.

Architects' fees vary according to the work involved. The scale of fees for a new house starts at 11.02 per cent for houses costing up to £57,137 and decreases to 9.9 per cent for houses costing from £57,137 to £142, 844. Fees for extensions are higher than for other building work, 'because it can be much more difficult to build on to an existing house and more complicated to alter it than to build a new house in an open field.' For extensions up to £57,137, the fee scale is 13.78 per cent for a full service; for bigger extensions it comes down somewhat. These fee bands are updated annually.

If you would like to find out more, the Royal Institute has a little booklet which describes precisely what an architect does, and you can buy it from them for £4. Write to the **Royal Institute of Architects of Ireland**, 8 Merrion Square North, Dublin 2, enclosing a cheque or postal order.

There is no actual scale of fees in Northern Ireland, but you can buy, for £3 sterling, a little booklet called *The Architect's Appointment*, which sets out, among other information, a recommended scale for fees and expenses. Essentially, the fees are very similar to those in the Republic of Ireland. You can get this booklet from the **Royal Society of Ulster Architects**, 2 Mount Charles, Belfast BT7 INZ, ☎ 0232 323760.

Architectural salvage (see building materials)

Architectural turnings:

James Harding Fireplaces, The Green, Gowran, Co. Kilkenny, ☎ 056 26177, do much more than just fireplaces. They construct architectural turnings, such as balustrades and door columns; in fact, they restored all the balustrades for the top of the Custom House in Dublin. They make old-style marble hand basins, kitchen worktops and bar counters – indeed, anything you want in stone, granite or marble.

• ariston appliances

Bluebell Appliance
Service Ltd
Naas Road
Dublin 12
☎ Dublin 783955/508455
(Republic of Ireland)

Merloni Domestic Appliances Ltd
35 Little Donegal Street
Belfast BT1 2JD
☎ 0232 242420
(*Northern Ireland*)

• asthma society of ireland

Asthma Society of Ireland
24 Anglesea Street
Dublin 2
☎ Dublin 716551

This society provides an asthma-information service for people who suffer from asthma and for the parents of asthmatic children. For an annual fee of £5, you can receive a forty-eight-page asthma-information booklet, as well as three issues a year of *Asthma Society News*, which has updated information on asthma treatment and research.

The Asthma Society is also happy to supply people with any information they have on products on the market which may help asthma patients. The list is quite an extensive one, but two products worth mentioning are the following.

Artilan: This is a special paint which is said to help asthma victims – it rids the house of dust mite. The idea is to apply it to all the paintable surfaces in the room of a patient who is allergic to dust mite. **David Burns** of **Fibreseal (Ireland) Ltd**, 8 Avondale Hall, Carysfort Avenue, Blackrock, Co. Dublin, ☎ Dublin 283 1444, is the agent for Artilan paint, which is available in matt emulsion, silk vinyl and gloss. Equally, David Burns supplies Banamite.

Banamite: An anti-allergenic spray, Banamite neutralises the antigens which cause allergic reactions – these include house dust mites, pollen, animal dander and feathers.

• back boilers

It has been said that a back boiler is never again as effective as the first time it is lit – when there is direct and unsullied contact between the fire and the new surface of the boiler. As it is used, however, a coating builds up on the boiler surface, which has to be regularly removed to get maximum efficiency from your fire. This is never a very nice job, and various gadgets have appeared on the market in recent years which claim to make the job easier. Usually they are scrapers of one kind or another, and some of them can be quite effective, but very hard work. **David White** of **White Leather Industries, Waterford**, however, is marketing a special chemical compound which genuinely does seem to help loosen the boiler build-up, making a dirty job much easier to do. Called **White's Cleaner**, it should be available in hardware shops and supermarkets around the country, but if you have any difficulty in getting it, telephone David White in Waterford at ☎ 051 70688.

• balay ovens and hobs

Appliance Care
Unit 4, Ballymount Drive
Ballymount Industrial Estate
Walkinstown
Dublin 12
☎ Dublin 502655
(*Republic of Ireland*)

For service outside of Dublin, ring this same number for the name and number of your local service agent.

Euro Serv (Ireland) Ltd
66 Dows Road
Drumbo
Belfast BT8 8LB
☎ 0232 826446
(*Northern Ireland*)

• barometers and barographs, repaired and restored

Cormac Kavanagh
18 Harcourt Road
Dublin 2
☎ Dublin 752184

Cormac worked for fourteen years with Masons, a very old Dublin firm which used to sell photographic, optical and laboratory supplies in Dame Street, Dublin. He set up on his own some twenty years ago. Cormac repairs aneroid and mercury barometers, barographs, thermographs and hygrographs, and binoculars and telescopes. He also sells this kind of equipment.

Edmund Ryan
67 Monastery Drive
Clondalkin
Dublin 22
☎ Dublin 591432

Edmund was an accountant for most of his life, but he was always an enthusiastic DIY man. For a number of years he has devoted his energies to restoring old barometers. He will also fit a quartz movement to an old clock – quite often people have a clock which doesn't work and can't be repaired in the usual way, but to which they have a sentimental attachment. Edmund will fit a quartz movement in the clock so that you can keep it and enjoy it.

Mark Causer
22b Magazine Road
Cork
☎ 021 311463

Mark repairs barometers and barographs, tide gauges for Cork County Council and makes parts for vintage cars. He also repairs clocks. He has a small machine workshop and can be a very useful man to know if you want some special or unusual piece individually made. Mark was in both the British and the Irish navy and today is a relief engineer on the Asgard 11, the well-known Irish civilian sail-training ship.

bathrooms

Installing or revamping a new bathroom can cost quite a lot of money, usually much more than you had envisaged spending in the beginning. So, cost out every detail, from the plumbing fittings and the nuts and bolts, right down to the finishing fittings, such as lavatory paper holders, mirrors, towel rails, shelving, wall heaters, and bathroom stools or seats – everything adds to the cost.

Before you make any decisions, shop around. There are a number of shops and showrooms you may like to visit, or firms you may like to consult, before you make any final decisions. Some of the big importers of sanitary ware have their own showrooms in Ireland. True, most of these tend to be in the Dublin area, but if you see something you like locally you might think it worth your while to visit the main showrooms to inspect the complete range before you make up your mind. Just remember that you can't *buy* in a distributor's showroom, they are not retail outlets; but if you see something you especially like you can order it through your local supplier.

Ideal Standard ware is imported into this country by **K. M. Reynolds**: their showroom is in Knockmitten Lane, off the Killeen Road, off the Naas Road, on the way into Dublin from the South, ☎ Dublin 520333. Just recently they opened a splendid new showroom at Erne Place, Holles Street, Dublin, with a first-class selection of bathroom ware and a variety of showers in operation. You can telephone them there at ☎ Dublin 764445.

Armitage Shanks (Ireland) Ltd have a showroom in Tallaght at Unit 1, Cookstown Industrial Estate, Dublin 24, ☎ Dublin 510044.

Shires (Ireland) Ltd have their showroom at Broomhill Road, also in Tallaght, ☎ Dublin 515877.

There are also a number of retail showrooms in Dublin which specialise in bathroom fittings and fitments, and which stock products from a variety of different manufacturers – in these showrooms you can look *and* buy.

Davis King is in Unit 4, the Pye Complex, Sandyford Road, Dublin 16, ☎ Dublin 2982828. Talk to Maurice Gibney, who is a fund of good, down-to-earth information. He says he sells 'affordable affluence'. He stocks modern designs and a selection of reproduction Victorian, Edwardian and Colonial suites.

Elegant John at Arcon, Herberton Road, Rialto, Dublin, ☎ Dublin 541384, do very upmarket bathrooms – splendid, but you're talking big money, definitely the luxury end of the trade. They are also located at New Street Mall, Malahide, Co. Dublin, ☎ Dublin 8451044.

Bathroom World is at 45 Lower Kevin Street, Dublin, opposite Kevin Street College, ☎ Dublin 784330/784614. They do reproduction and modern suites and a good range of accessories.

Bathroom Boutique in 5 South Leinster Street, near Merrion Square, Dublin, ☎ Dublin 762061, do bathroom suites and bathroom accessories.

As well, there are a number of builders' providers and plumbing outlets, which offer a good selection of bathroom ware. Among them are the following.

F. & T. Buckley Ltd
Robinhood Road
Clondalkin
Dublin 22
☎ Dublin 507770

Chadwicks Ltd
Greencastle Parade
Coolock
Dublin 5
☎ Dublin 8475733

Chadwicks Ltd
Dublin Industrial Estate
Glasnevin
Dublin 11
☎ Dublin 307811

Chadwicks Ltd
Sallynoggin Road
Sallynoggin
Co. Dublin
☎ Dublin 2851233

Chadwicks Ltd
Sandyford Industrial Estate
Sandyford
Dublin 18
☎ Dublin 2954601

Chadwicks Ltd
Lucan
Co. Dublin
☎ Dublin 6282122

Davies
6/8 Richmond Avenue
Fairview
Dublin 3
☎ Dublin 376076

Dublin Providers Ltd
68 Old Kilmainham
Dublin 8
☎ Dublin 531046

Euro Heating & Plumbing Supplies Ltd
3 Beechlawn Industrial Complex
Greenhills Road
Dublin 12
☎ Dublin 502933

H. & V. Centre
North Road
Finglas
Dublin 11
☎ Dublin 345457

Joseph Kelly & Sons Ltd
66 Thomas Street
Dublin 8
☎ Dublin 542200

P. H. Ross Ltd
16 Old Cabra Road
Dublin 7
☎ Dublin 385666

Southside Builders Merchants
2a Convent Road
Dun Laoghaire
Co. Dublin
☎ Dublin 2843494

Smiths Building Supplies
Greenhills Road
Tallaght
Dublin 12
☎ Dublin 508056

Tubs and Tiles
1 Kylemore Road
Dublin 10
☎ Dublin 6264493/6264495

You may not want a new bathroom, you may just want it repaired or restored.

New baths for old:

If you have an old cast-iron bath which is looking the worse for wear, it can be re-enamelled very successfully, in white or in a number of other colours. However, you must obey the instructions and not use the bath for a week to allow the enamel to 'cure' – and be sure to get any dripping taps mended before the job is done. The people who do the enamelling are listed below.

Renubath
139 St Peter's Road
Walkinstown
Dublin 12
☎ Dublin 500433
(Republic of Ireland)

Bathglaze
158-160 Union Street
Lurgan
Craigavon
Co. Armagh BT66 8EQ
☎ 0762 326655
(*Northern Ireland*)

Bathroom replacements:

R. T. Large & Sons
Spitalsfields
Francis Street
Dublin 8
☎ Dublin 541699/541760
(replace individual pieces)

If you have a coloured suite in your bathroom, and one piece gets damaged, you may think you have to replace the whole suite as it can be difficult to get individual matching pieces. If, however, your suite is turquoise, sky blue, primrose, pink, avocado, burgundy or pampas, you will be delighted to know that basins, pedestals, toilet pans, cisterns, bidets and even baths are available individually in these colours from **R. T. Large**. If you live in the Republic outside Dublin, telephone them for the name of your nearest stockist.

In Northern Ireland contact **Mr J. Cathers, JJC Agencies**, Unit 1a, Campsie Real Estate, McClean Road, Eglington, Co. Londonderry BT47 3PF, ☎ 0504 860953.

Bathroom fittings:

You may have a fitting, even a very old one, which needs replacing, and you may find it difficult to get the one you need. Chances are you'll obtain it in **Smallmans**, 3 Bachelor's Way, off Bachelor's Walk, Dublin, ☎ Dublin 732510. Dermott McNeice, who runs Smallmans, has a huge stock of old fittings, and if you don't find what you're looking for there, you probably won't get it at all.

Bathroom showrooms to visit outside Dublin:

Carlow:

R. N. Gillespie Ltd
Kennedy Avenue
Carlow
☎ 0503 31647

Clare:

Ennis Supply Co. Ltd
Gort Road
Ennis
Co. Clare
☎ 065 21141

Cork:

Buckleys Ltd
Ardarostig
Bishopstown
Co. Cork
☎ 021 544099

Chadwicks Ltd
Coolbawn
Midleton
Co. Cork
☎ 021 631311

Chadwicks Ltd
Shortcastle Road
Mallow
Co. Cork
☎ 022 21844

Cork Builders' Providers Ltd
Casey's Cross
Pouladuff Road
Cork
☎ 021 961700

Dublin Providers Ltd
Kinsale Road
Clarkesbridge
Cork
☎ 021 964955

Heating and Plumbing Centre Ltd
12 Cornmarket Street
Cork
☎ 021 277290

Hickey (Cork) Ltd
9-12 Maylor Street
Cork
☎ 021 273281

Irish International Trading Corporation
Rocksavage
Co. Cork
☎ 021 275161

O. B. Heating and Plumbing Supplies
St Patrick's Mills
Douglas
Cork
☎ 021 362431

The Shower Shop
Rocksavage
Anglesea Street
Cork
☎ 021 962914

Tubs and Tiles
5 Penrose Quay
Cork
☎ 021 506944

Galway:

Buckleys Builders' Providers
Wellpark
Galway
☎ 091 53220

Morahan & Hughes Ltd
Tuam Road
Galway
☎ 091 51862

T. O' Higgins & Co. Ltd
Shantalla
Galway
☎ 091 22411

Walsh's Heating and Plumbing Supplies
Tuam Road
Galway
☎ 091 57248

Kerry:

P. & T. Fitzgerald & Co.
Main Street
Dingle
Co. Kerry
☎ 066 51177

O'Callaghan Bros. Ltd
College Street
Killarney
Co. Kerry
☎ 064 31175

M. D. O'Shea & Sons Ltd
Main Street
Killarney
Co. Kerry
☎ 064 31029

Kildare:

Chadwicks Ltd
Newbridge Road
Naas
Co. Kildare
☎ 045 76711

M. & A. Heating and Plumbing Supplies Ltd
Unit 12, Tarmel Centre
Cutlery Road
Newbridge
Co. Kildare
☎ 045 31600

Kilkenny:

Chadwicks Ltd
Hebron Road
Kilkenny
☎ 056 21044

Tubs and Tiles
Industrial Estate
Hebron Road
Kilkenny
☎ 056 62244

Limerick:

A. & R. Supplies
Roxtown Terrace
Lelia Street
Limerick
☎ 061 413321

Abbey Heating and Plumbing
Tipperary Road
Ballysimon
Co. Limerick
☎ 061 413722

J. P. Newsom and Co.
William Street
Limerick
☎ 061 414211

Shannonside Heating & Plumbing
Mulgrave Street
Limerick
☎ 061 412566

Tubs and Tiles
Roxboro
Limerick
☎ 061 311206

Louth:

Home Improvement Centre
Francis Street
Dundalk
Co. Louth
☎ 042 36912

Mayo:

Chadwicks Ltd
Newport Road
Castlebar
Co. Mayo
☎ 094 21077

Heiton McFerran Ltd
Industrial Estate
Castlebar
Co. Mayo
☎ 094 21377

Tony Scott Heating and Plumbing Supplies
Peter Street
Westport
☎ 098 25442

Meath:

Chadwicks Ltd
Carriage Road
Navan
Co. Meath
☎ 046 21999

Offaly:

Heatwise (Tullamore) Ltd
Cloncollig
Church Road
Tullamore
Co. Offaly
☎ 0506 51207

Walsh Bros. Plumbing and Heating Supplies
Killeigh
Tullamore
Co. Offaly
☎ 0506 54229

Roscommon:

Garveys Ltd
Castle Street
Roscommon
☎ 0903 26293

Sligo:

Brooks Hanley Ltd
Finisklin Road
Sligo
☎ 071 61111

Buckleys Ltd
Finisklin Road
Sligo
☎ 071 61701

A. M. Murray Ltd
Quay Street
Sligo
☎ 071 61474

Tubs and Tiles
Castle Street
Sligo
☎ 071 70325

Tipperary:

Chadwicks Ltd
Queen Street
Clonmel
Co. Tipperary
☎ 052 21822

Chadwicks Ltd
Dublin Road
Nenagh
Co. Tipperary
☎ 067 32088

Clonmel Plumbing Supplies
21 Upper Irishtown
Clonmel
Co. Tipperary
☎ 052 23422

Waterford:

Paddy Power Plumbing and Heating
Carigward
Six Cross Roads
Waterford
☎ 051 78944

Tubs and Tiles
Park Road
Waterford
☎ 051 77304

Westmeath:

Chadwicks Ltd
Dublin Road
Athlone
Co. Westmeath
☎ 0902 72751

Tubs and Tiles
Deerpark Road
Athlone
Co. Westmeath
☎ 0902 92755

Wexford:

Liam Brennan Ltd
Market Square
Gorey
Co. Wexford
☎ 055 20244

Chadwicks Ltd
Trinity Street
Wexford
☎ 053 23699

Dublin Providers Ltd
Commercial Quay
Wexford
☎ 053 23977

Wicklow:

Heiton McFerran Ltd
Castle Street
Bray
Co. Wicklow
☎ Dublin 2867621

In Northern Ireland, showrooms include the following.

Armatile Ltd
Boucher Crescent
Belfast BT12 6HU
☎ 0232 682752

Armatile Ltd
Station Road
Armagh BT61 7NT
☎ 0861 527007

Bassets Heating and Plumbing
Mahon Industrial Estate
Mahon Road
Portadown BT62 3EH
☎ 0762 339438

Beggs & Partners
Pennybridge Industrial Estate
Larne Road
Ballymena BT42 3HB
☎ 0266 45121

Central Merchants (Northern Ireland) Ltd
Nelson Trade Centre
Nelson Street
Belfast BT15 1BH
☎ 0232 329767

Clady Plumbing Supplies Ltd
37 Glenone Road
Clady
Portglenone BT44 8LD
☎ 0266 821448

Elite Bathrooms
Bushmills Road
Coleraine BT52 2NX
☎ 0265 44552

J. Frackleton & Sons Ltd
25 Imperial Drive
Belfast BT6 8JH
☎ 0232 732231

Glenhill Merchants Ltd
Musgrave Park Industrial Estate
Stockman's Way
Belfast BT9 7ET
☎ 0232 669444

Haldane, Fisher (North Down) Ltd
41a Bangor Road
Conlig
Newtownards BT23 3PX
☎ 0247 271711

Haldane, Fisher Ltd
Carnbane Industrial Estate
Shepherd's Way
Newry BT35 6QJ
☎ 0693 63201

Robin Irvine Ltd
61 Boucher Road
Belfast BT12 6HR
☎ 0232 665611

John McCandless Ltd
Loguestown Industrial Estate
Bushmills Road
Coleraine BT52 2NP
☎ 0265 44422

Plumb Center
2-5 Whitla Street
Belfast BT15 1JP
☎ 0232 751626

Plumb Center
Lisburn Commercial Centre
Lisburn BT27 5EA
☎ 0846 602121

Price & Hughes Ltd
Millar Street
Belfast BT6 8JZ
☎ 0232 453720

Shawmac Ltd
Batchelor's Walk
Lisburn BT28 1XN
☎ 0846 602216

T. A. Shillington & Son Ltd
Castle Street
Portadown BT62 1BD
☎ 0762 337321

Stevenson & Reid Ltd
8 Abbey Trading Estate
Longwood Road
Newtownabbey BT36 7PA
☎ 0232 852212

Stevenson & Reid Ltd
34 Cullybackey Road
Ballymena BT43 5DF
☎ 0266 49715

Stevenson & Reid Ltd
Ballybrakes Industrial Estate
Ballymoney BT53 6LQ
☎ 02656 65094

Stevenson & Reid Ltd
12 Orritor Street
Cookstown BT80 8BE
☎ 06487 62199

Paul Thompson Heating & Plumbing
35 Waringstown Road
Lurgan BT66 7HH
☎ 0762 881407

W. J. Thompson (E) Ltd
Carrigans
Sligo Road
Enniskillen BT74 7JZ
☎ 0365 323888

• bauknecht appliances

Philips and Whirlpool Major Appliances
Unit 4, Allied Industrial Estate
Kylemore Road
Dublin 10
☎ Dublin 6231013
(*Republic of Ireland*)

Euro Serv (Ireland) Ltd
66 Dows Road
Drumbo
Belfast BT8 8LB
☎ 0232 826446
(*Northern Ireland*)

• baumatic ovens and hobs

Robert Johnston
377b Antrim Road
Glengormley
Newtownabbey BT36 8EB
☎ 0232 342558

• bean bag patterns

Singer Sewing and Craft Centre
54 Capel Street
Dublin 1
☎ Dublin 730623

Michael Gordon stocks patterns for bean bags, as well as a wide range of other craft and sewing materials.

beds

Buying:

When you go out to buy a new bed, choose carefully. A nice floral cover may immediately appeal, but it is what's under the cover that counts, and unless you buy a reputable make of bed from an established retailer, and a good brand, you cannot always be sure of what's under that cover.

Try out the bed – don't just sit on it, lie on it. Many people feel inhibited about doing this, but you're the one who is going to be sleeping on it for a number of years. A good retailer will encourage you to test the bed in order to be sure you're buying the right one for you.

Orthopaedic beds:

The word 'orthopaedic' can be used freely where beds are concerned. Sometimes the word has real meaning, sometimes it hasn't. The **King Koil** beds made by **Kayfoam Woolfson** in Dublin (they also make O'Dearest beds) were designed in America in conjunction with the International Chiropractic Association and are made here under licence (chiropractors are specialists in the treatment of back problems). This is not to say that other orthopaedic beds are not good – just check the credentials before you buy.

bees, getting rid of

If you have an uninvited swarm of bees in your garden, the people to contact are your local beekeepers. There are always beekeepers looking for swarms. If you don't know how to find your local association, **Tom Kehoe** is the man to contact – he gets regular calls from people both in Dublin and further afield who very definitely *don't* want the swarm which arrived in their garden. You can reach **Tom Kehoe** at 106 North Circular Road, Dublin 7, ☎ Dublin 386609.

bee-keeping

If you want to find out about bees and bee-keeping, the best people to talk to are local beekeepers or the local beekeepers' association – beekeepers are always delighted to welcome and encourage newcomers. If you don't know who they are, probably the best person to contact is **Tom Kehoe** – as below, Dublin ☎ 386609 – who supplies beekeepers all over the country and always has a current list of local associations and their acting secretaries.

Equipment and supplies:

Thomas J. Kehoe
106 North Circular Road
Dublin 7
☎ Dublin 386609

Aitkins Garden World
6 Camden Quay
Cork
☎ 021 502473

belling appliances

Parts:

Charlie Shiels
Golden Bridge Industrial Estate
Inchicore
Dublin 8
☎ Dublin 545844

Service:

Dimpco Ltd
Airport Road
Cloghran
Dublin 9
☎ Dublin 8428222

In Northern Ireland contact the following supplier.

Homecare Appliance Service
Abbey Trading Estate
Longwood Road
Newtownabbey
Belfast BT36 7LD
☎ 0232 365487

be modern fire surrounds

Brownbrook Distributors Ltd
Unit 24, Seagoe Industrial Estate
Portadown
Co. Armagh BT63 5TH
☎ 0762 337317

bendix appliances

Service:

Electroservice
Long Mile Road
Dublin 12
☎ Dublin 518666

Parts:

Charlie Shiels
Golden Bridge Industrial Estate
Inchicore
Dublin 8
☎ Dublin 545844
(*Republic of Ireland*)

Electrolux Tricity Bendix Service
Unit 3, Edenderry Industrial Estate
326 Crumlin Road
Belfast BT14 7EE
☎ 0232 746591
(*Northern Ireland*)

berry magicoal heaters

Beaumark Service Company Ltd
2a Sunbury Industrial Estate
Dublin 12
☎ Dublin 504620
(*Republic of Ireland*)

Domestic Sales and Repair Services Ltd
219 Kingsway
Dunmurry
Belfast BT17 9SB
☎ 0232 301533
(*Northern Ireland*)

Or you can contact **CareElectric.** CareElectric in Northern Ireland is a province-wide network of experienced service electricians, co-ordinated by mobile telephone to the headquarters of Northern Ireland Electricity. They are on call Monday to Friday and you can telephone them from anywhere in Northern Ireland at the local rate. The number to ring is ☎ 0345 616744.

• binoculars (see barometers)

Cormac Kavanagh
18 Harcourt Road
Dublin 2
☎ Dublin 752184

• bins on wheels

Tank Engineering, Industrial Estate Blessington, Co. Wicklow, ☎ 045 65044 makes them. These bins can now be seen in various parts of the country. They are ideally used with bin collection vans specially equipped to lift the entire bin and empty it in one operation, and they are kind to binmen and the householder alike – the bin can be wheeled instead of carried. They are sometimes supplied by local authorities.

• bissell carpet and vacuum cleaners

Ideal Service
Kylemore Park West
Ballyfermot
Dublin 10
☎ Dublin 6266720

• black and decker

Black and Decker
14–15 Parliament Street
Dublin 10
☎ Dublin 777177

Cork Power Tools
43 Douglas Street
Cork
☎ 021 311472

Electrical Rewind Services
23 Roches Street
Limerick
☎ 061 417444

Denis Long Electrical Ltd
Rock Street
Tralee
Co. Kerry
☎ 066 23022

Euro Electronics Ltd
10 Abbey Shopping Centre
Drogheda
☎ 041 39600

In Northern Ireland Black and Decker appliances can be obtained at the following address.

Black and Decker
232 Antrim Road
Glengormley
Newtownabbey BT36 7QX
☎ 0232 841071/2

black tissue paper

Acid-free black tissue paper is recommended for wrapping white materials, such as first communion dresses, wedding dresses and christening robes.

K. & M. Evans
28 Mary's Abbey
Dublin 7
☎ Dublin 726855

You should never, ever store a white wedding dress, a first communion dress or a christening robe in a plastic bag. The white material will turn yellow. Put the garment into a cardboard box, layer black tissue paper underneath it, fold the skirt on to the tissue paper, put another layer of tissue paper over it, then fold in the top and cover it with the paper. Alternatively, you can hang the dress in your wardrobe, pinning sheets of tissue paper together around it, and then perhaps pin an old sheet around it as well.

• blaupunkt equipment

Beaver Engineering Ltd
Greenhills Road
Tallaght
Dublin 24
☎ Dublin 515211
(*Republic of Ireland*)

John Robertson (Belfast) Ltd
69 Glenmachan Street
Belfast BT12 6JB
☎ 0232 232066
(*Northern Ireland*)

• blomberg appliances

Ideal Service
Kylemore Park West
Ballyfermot
Dublin 10
☎ Dublin 6266720

Blomberg customers in Northern Ireland are also looked after by Ideal Service from Dublin, as above.

• bodhráns, repaired

Malachy Kearns
Roundstone Musical Instruments
Michael Killeen Craft Centre
Roundstone
Co. Galway
☎ 095 35808

Malachy makes new bodhráns and repairs old ones.

bookbinding and restoration

Des Breen is deeply committed to the revival of the old craft of hand bookbinding. He restores old and precious books to their original beauty and makes special bindings for special editions of modern books. Books come to his workshop from famous libraries and private collections. You'll find **Des Breen** in **Antiquarian Bookcrafts Ltd**, Marley Craft Courtyard, Marlay Park, Grange Road, Dublin 16, ☎ Dublin 942834.

Archbishop Marsh's Library, beside St Patrick's Cathedral, is one of the most famous libraries in Dublin, a treasure house of old and rare books. The Delmas Bindery in the library restores and repairs old books. You can contact the **Delmas Bindery** in **Archbishop Marsh's Library**, St Patrick's Close, Dublin 8, ☎ Dublin 544609/543511.

• bosch

Power tools:

Beaver Engineering Ltd
Greenhills Road
Tallaght
Co. Dublin
☎ Dublin 515211
(*Republic of Ireland*)

Robert Craig & Sons Ltd
19 Great George's Street
Belfast BT15 1BP
☎ 0232 232971
(*Northern Ireland*)

Domestic appliances:

Appliance Care
Unit 4, Ballymount Drive
Ballymount Industrial Estate
Walkinstown
Dublin 12
☎ Dublin 502655
(*Republic of Ireland*)

Euro Serv (Ireland) Ltd
66 Dows Road
Drumbo
Belfast BT8 8LB
☎ 0232 826446
(*Northern Ireland*)

brass

James Healy, Founders and Engineers, 51a Pearse Street, Dublin 2, ☎ Dublin 772238, have been in business for over fifty years. They are stockholders of brass, bronze, copper and aluminium in all shapes and sizes and in a variety of different forms – sheets, tubes, rods, bars and profiles. You can buy in Dublin or from their warehouses in Monaghan Road, Cork, ☎ 021 964111; Greenpark, South Circular Road, Limerick, ☎ 061 28055; and James Street, Claremorris, Co. Mayo, ☎ 094 71178. Off-cuts of brass are sometimes available and are very good value for the small craftworker.

In Dublin Healy's have a fabrication shop where they do architectural metal work to detailed plans provided by builders, architects and surveyors. There is also a repair service available in Dublin where they restore, repair, polish and lacquer all kinds of metal items, including many domestic pieces. A polishing service is available in Cork.

City Brass
73/74 Francis Street
Dublin 8
☎ Dublin 542696

Kevin Nolan of **City Brass** has been in business for over thirty years. He restores and repairs every kind of brass piece, including old lamps, and polishes, fits extra bits and lacquers. He retails as well as repairs, and says that all the pieces he sells are genuinely old – he doesn't sell any reproductions.

Billy Potter
Dublin Art Metals
37 Summerhill Parade
Dublin 1
☎ Dublin 743729

Billy specialises in one-off brass pieces – if you have an antique or an old piece of brass which is missing a part, Billy will make it for you. He also makes lamp stands, grids and grills, fire irons and fenders, and does filigree brasswork.

Donal Gallagher of **Brasscraft Ltd**, Ballycurreen, Kinsale Road, Cork, ☎ 021 317373, specialises in the repair and restoration of brass. Donal Gallagher was one of a number of skilled craftsmen who worked for the firm of William Egan in Cork, now, alas, no more. Egan's employed craftsmen specialising in a variety of different areas and had a prestigious reputation for high-quality work. They were, essentially, ecclesiastical suppliers and furnished the needs of churches, both Catholic and Protestant, and religious orders all over Ireland. They had a cabinet-making workshop which made church furniture, a clock-making department, a vestment room, a jewellery workshop, and they specialised in church plate.

In 1951 Donal Gallagher began in the Egan's cabinet-making department and went on to work with brass, silver and gold. He says he learned a lot in Egan's, with whom he remained until 1971. 'I learned how to be versatile. You had to use your imagination, and if you weren't gifted with your hands and hadn't some brains, you'd never get on. You had to have talent. A great number of very talented people worked in Egan's.'

It was all good training. When Donal set up on his own he found he was able to adapt himself to all kinds of work. 'I could take on anything that came in. I learned versatility in Egan's because you have the opportunity of working in different materials and in different workshops. As well, they had a designer who was very good. He designed all the work we carried out in Egan's. There was always excitement, always something going on. You were given ideas and you had to be creative. There was never a dull moment.'

Donal particularly remembers the time President Kennedy came to Cork. 'We had to make a silver casket for the scroll which gave him the freedom of the city.' The scroll was laboured on by silversmiths, jewellers, woodworkers – as in Donal's case – and engravers. 'It was a splendid piece of work, solid silver, and everybody came together to work on it.'

Working at first with wood, Donal has made the transition to metal and today specialises mainly in brass. He refurbishes churches, occasionally making pieces, and restores all kinds of domestic brass. Beds are a particular speciality. Old cast-iron and brass beds have become very popular, and Donal clearly enjoys making them look like new. 'We get beds that have come out of old cowsheds and old barns, beds that have come out of ditches where they've been used to stop a gap. They're coming from all kinds of places. We strip them down, sandblast them, paint the ironwork, polish up the brass parts, and you wouldn't believe how good they can look. Sometimes a customer may have only one end of a bed, but we can make up the other end to match.'

As well, people bring Donal their house ornaments, coal scuttles and fenders, and ask him to make fire frames, canopies or hoods, or bring him old ones to repair. They bring door furniture – knobs and knockers and letter-boxes – and he cleans and repairs them. Many pieces he lacquers. 'Lacquering doesn't take from a piece, it just makes it easier to keep clean. You don't have to polish it every day, just wipe it over from time to time.'

Cork Brass & Gift
8 Liberty Street
Cork
☎ 021 274961

This is a retail shop with a full range of everything you could want in brass, from door knobs and knockers and letter-boxes, to log-boxes, fenders, fire screens and the full range of giftware. Some they make themselves, some they import. They will also make special pieces to order, and polish and lacquer old pieces. They do a lot of bar and restaurant work.

Murphy & Quinlan
19 Lavitt's Quay
Cork
☎ 021 271418

John Murphy restores and refurbishes brass and copper and makes pieces to order. He also does quite a bit of work for bars and restaurants.

Ion White of **Brass Beds**, Coachhouse Beds, Ballymore Eustace, Co. Kildare, ☎ 045 64121, has a comprehensive range of Victorian beds, all genuine antiques and painstakingly restored. They range from simple cast iron to decorative cast iron and brass, to all-brass beds. He's open seven days a week.

brasso

Brasso is very good for polishing brass pieces, but don't overdo it. We once had a major culinary catastrophe in our house involving Brasso. We were expecting very special visitors to dinner, relatives who hadn't visited Ireland or our home for a number of years, and we were determined to prepare a really nice meal. And I personally was determined to have everything ready, not only in time but in advance, although I find it difficult to do *anything* in time, never mind in advance.

We spent a considerable part of the day trying to clean the house and squabbling over who did what. There are always jobs that nobody really wants to do – bathrooms, windows or washing floors. With the cleaning underway, I turned to cooking. It was one of the relatively rare occasions when I had actually done some preparation work the night before. I was feeling quite pleased with myself.

For the main course we were having a chicken casserole, and because it was such a special occasion, I decided to buy chicken breasts; one of my ideas of real luxury has always been a casserole made solely of chicken breasts. Nobody was going to get an excess of chicken, but the recipe also had sherry, peppers, onions, raisins, tomatoes and black olives in it. Since there are ten of us and we were expecting seven visitors, that added up to a considerable amount of chicken and demanded quite a big casserole.

The casserole I normally use wasn't big enough, so I had to take down a big brass preserving pan which I rarely cook in. Naturally, it wasn't polished, and naturally we had to polish it – we did, until it absolutely gleamed. I rinsed it out, very carefully I thought, with washing-up liquid and warm water, wiped it and turned the casserole ingredients into it, accompanied by a generous cup of sherry, leaving it to cook.

It was when I went to taste it for seasoning that the full flavour hit me – Brasso. I called one daughter to sample it; her face said Brasso. I asked a friend and a second daughter: Brasso. I tasted it again myself, not wanting to believe the evidence of my own taste buds. There was no doubt about it – the flavour was very definitely Brasso. In my efforts to wash the inside of the pan without interfering with the gleam of the outside, I'd obviously left some vestiges of polish behind.

'Try putting a load of garlic into it', said my eldest daughter, and we added another nine or ten cloves to the ones which had already gone in.

'Try putting some more sherry into it', said one of my sons, so I emptied the best part of the bottle into it.

'Try putting some tomato purée into it', said my youngest daughter, so we emptied two tins of purée into it. The Brasso won out over the lot.

'Try throwing it out,' said another son, 'unless you want to poison the lot of us.' I was appalled at the enormity of the disaster, but I couldn't quite bring myself to throw it all out. I transferred it to an old pot and left it on the worktop until I had more time to think about it.

I now had about three hours to go shopping – twelve miles away – buy more ingredients and start all over again. Whatever else was to be said about the recipe, at least it was fairly simple, and by the time the guests arrived we had the casserole safely in the oven. This time I washed and rinsed and rinsed and washed the casserole, and said to blazes with the shine. And while association of ideas meant that everything now seemed to taste of Brasso, I knew this was purely my imagination.

What was not my imagination, however, was the original lot of Brassoed chicken in the old pot sitting on the worktop, which was the first thing that met my eye the following morning. So what was I going to do with it? Clearly nobody was going to eat it, but how was I going to dispose of it? I thought about putting it in the dustbin, but I knew that the scent of so much chicken would bring every fox for miles along to root – and probably our own dog and cats wouldn't be far behind. And we'd end up with the contents of the bin all over the driveway. I debated flushing it away in the bathroom, but decided that this would be asking a bit much of our plumbing system and the septic tank. I decided that it should be buried in the garden, but nobody seemed very enthusiastic about taking on this project. The dog would only dig it up, I was told, or the cats.

Finally, I decided that it should be carried out into the forest, *far* out into the forest, and disposed of there. There are 120 acres of forestry around our house, and it should surely be possible to lose even that much Brassoed chicken out there. 'What about the wildlife', said one of my daughters in shocked tones. 'Don't you care about them?' I said that at the very most there could only be the merest *trace* of Brasso in it, which would probably not be noticeable to the animals. I persuaded my youngest son to carry it off and lose it, and when he came back and assured me he had done a good job, I didn't inquire too closely. I can't believe that the trace of Brasso could have done any animals any harm – though they might well have suffered a hangover from the amount of sherry in it.

• braun shavers and kitchen appliances

Gavins Shaver Centre
83 Lower Camden Street
Dublin 2
☎ Dublin 757109
(*Republic of Ireland*)

Domestic Sales and Repair Services Ltd
219 Kingsway
Dunmurry
Belfast BT17 9SB
☎ 0232 301533
(*Northern Ireland*)

• breville appliances

Noel McCabe Distributors
Bluebell Industrial Estate
Dublin 12
☎ Dublin 502926
(*Republic of Ireland*)

Domestic Sales and Repair Services
219 Kingsway
Dunmurry
Belfast BT17 9SB
☎ 0232 301533

P. Laverty
61a Ballymacombs Road
Portglennone
Ballymena
Co. Antrim BT44 8NT
☎ 064 886263
(*Northern Ireland*)

• brill lawnmowers

Noel McCabe Distributors
Bluebell Industrial Estate
Dublin 12
☎ Dublin 502926

• brother appliances

Brother International (Ireland) Ltd
Airways Industrial Estate
Boeing Road, Santry
Dublin 17
☎ Dublin 8424777
(*Republic of Ireland*)

Sewing and knitting machines:

Sew-Knit Machine Centre
26 Bridge Street
Lisburn BT28 1XY
☎ 0846 601200

Microwave ovens:

K. T. Distributors
Unit 2, Balloo Crescent
Balloo Industrial Estate
Bangor
Co. Down BT19 2YX
☎ 0247 270130
(*Northern Ireland*)

• building materials, old

If you are refurbishing an old house and need genuine old materials to do the job properly, or if you like old materials and want to incorporate them in any building project, you should visit the following.

Architectural Salvage and Supplies
19 South Gloucester Street
Dublin 2
☎ Dublin 551299

Mark McDonagh at Architectural Salvage and Supplies has pier and wall cappings, cobblestones, old bricks, quarry tiles and slates, old panelling and pews, old doors and etched glass, old baths, sinks and lavatories, leaded lights and handrails, and many other interesting items.

Edward Byrne
Deerfield, Paulville
Tullow
Co. Carlow
☎ 0503 51750

Edward prefers the word 'reclamation' to 'salvage' and says he is in the business of 'traditional building materials'. He is quite passionate about the right materials being used in the right place, and very knowledgeable about *how* they should be used and where. He has old granite sills and pier cappings; decorative granite and limestone pieces for the garden, including lovely, old water troughs; old stone paving and chimney pots; old Victorian and Georgian bricks; old windows, doors and shutters; and old architraving and floorboards.

• burco boilers, servicing

Dimpco Ltd
Airport Road
Cloghran
Dublin 9
☎ Dublin 8428222

In Northern Ireland contact Brownbrook Distributors for the name of your nearest service person.

Brownbrook Distributors Ltd
Unit 24, Seagoe Industrial Estate
Portadown
Co. Armagh BT63 5TH
☎ 0762 337317

• camping

If you want to hire out a tent or a travel cot or a fridge, you can hire them from **O'Meara Camping** at 26 Ossory Road, North Strand, Dublin 3, ☎ Dublin 363233 – they're in the Ossory Business Park.

• candy appliances

Ideal Service
Kylemore Park West
Ballyfermot
Dublin 10
☎ Dublin 6266720
(*Republic of Ireland*)

Robert Johnston
377b Antrim Road
Glengormley
Newtownabbey BT36 8EB
☎ 0232 342558
(*Northern Ireland*)

• canon gas cookers

Canon gas cookers run on Calor Kosangas, and there is a big network of service agents around the country. Any dealer stockist will have a list. If you can't find one, contact **Calor Kosangas**, Long Mile Road, Dublin 12, ☎ Dublin 505000.

If your cooker is run on Flogas Ergas, contact **Flogas Ergas Ltd**, Dublin Road, Drogheda, Co. Louth, ☎ 041 31041. If it is run on natural gas, contact your local gas company.

In Northern Ireland contact the following companies.

Calor Gas (Northern Ireland) Ltd
Airport Road West
Sydenham
Belfast BT3 9EE
☎ 0232 458466
(cookers run on Calor Kosangas)

Flogas (Northern Ireland) Ltd
Airport Road West
Belfast BT3 9ED
☎ 0232 732611
(cookers run on Flogas Ergas)

• caravell refrigerators, freezers and bottle coolers

Noel McCabe Distributors
Bluebell Industrial Estate
Dublin 12
☎ Dublin 502926

Caravell equipment is also serviced by Noel McCabe in Northern Ireland, from Dublin – address as above.

car keys

If you lose your car keys in Dublin and find yourself locked out, you can call **Steve Guard.** Steve operates a twenty-four-hour service, making on-the-spot replacements. It is sometimes possible to change the combination of the lock and provide new keys, rather than buy a whole new set of locks for your door – this can be quite a saving.

If your car has a burglar alarm, Steve can get you in without damaging the alarm. Your car may have a high-security deadlock, and when you go back to it you may find a thief has tried to break into the car, failed, but damaged the lock in the process so that you cannot unlock your own car. Steve can pass the deadlock and provide you with a new set of keys. The cost of the service varies according to the type of lock on the car. Steve operates in the Dublin area only and can be reached at ☎ 088 554848 or, in an emergency, at his home number, ☎ Dublin 364518. Take a note of the numbers. You might need them sometime.

• carmen appliances

Appliance Network Services Ltd
19 East Essex Street
Dublin 2
☎ Dublin 6795244/715528
(Republic of Ireland)

Teska Ltd
16 Cedarhurst Road
Newtownbreda
Belfast BT8 4RH
☎ 0232 644821
(Northern Ireland)

carpets

Buying:

Buying a carpet means spending quite a lot of money, so it is only common sense to think carefully before you make a final decision. Obviously, you will hope to live with that carpet for a long time, and you will want it to stand up to the rigours of everyday living.

Most of us have to think seriously about how much we can afford to spend, but cost should not be the primary consideration. Quality should be the priority when it comes to carpet buying. You want a carpet that will not only look good when it goes down, but continue to look good for many years – a carpet that will be easy to maintain, attractive to look at and resistant to minor accidents. A carpet which seems cheap initially may turn out to be quite expensive if you have to replace it in a few years' time. Buy the best you can afford, even if it means waiting a while and saving up. And the best carpet to buy is a wool carpet, or a carpet that is at least 80 per cent wool.

Wool carpets look better and keep their appearance longer than synthetic ones. It's not that a synthetic carpet wears out fast; in fact, most synthetic carpets *don't* wear out in this way. But they do go flat and dead looking and lose their appearance more easily, since they don't have the natural resilience of wool. They will also show spillages and stains more readily and don't bounce back as quickly from the assaults of everyday life as wool does.

One of the great advantages of wool in carpets is that its moisture content rises and falls with the weather and humidity. A wool carpet after heavy wear may look a bit grubby, but if you vacuum it on a good, airy, dry day when the moisture in the atmosphere is low, it is amazing how wool loses its soil and looks as though it has just been professionally cleaned.

When you go out to buy, you will have to decide whether you want a plain or a patterned carpet. In recent years the trend has been towards plainer, completely plain or semi-plain carpets. Plain carpets make it easier to furnish the rest of the room, and it's always simpler to change your curtains or your covers than to change your carpet. On the other hand, in a heavy-duty area, like the stairs or living-room, you may feel that a patterned carpet is more practical. But if you're buying a patterned carpet, don't buy one with too big or bright or obvious a pattern – you'll get to hate it after a few years. A reasonably discreet all-over pattern is a better purchase.

Colours are always important, and some show dirt and soil less than others. Dark green is good; dark red is not so good because it tends to show up footprints and dust marks. Beiges, biscuits, toffee and coffee colours are good. White carpets, delicate pastel carpets, pale blue and yellow carpets are probably unwise if you have a houseful of children.

Cleaning:

There is absolutely no doubt that if you have an expensive carpet and it needs cleaning, or has suffered a bad spillage, the best people to call in are professional cleaners. Consider the cost of replacing it, and the cost of cleaning won't seem so much. Having said that, the next question is where do you find good and reliable carpet cleaners? And that is the $64,000 question. There is nothing to stop anybody from buying the machinery and setting up in the carpet-cleaning business – and many people do. This does not mean that they have the qualifications or the knowledge or the experience, or that they have any training *at all* in how to clean carpets properly. Very many don't. So be warned.

There are, however, some people who are very conscientious and who have a completely professional approach to carpet cleaning. They include the following.

Ronnie Butler
Ideal Cleaning Services Ltd
Monkstown Farm
Dun Laoghaire
Co. Dublin
☎ Dublin 2801458

Ronnie can wax lyrical on the subject of cleaning.

Bob Ryan
Busy Bee Carpet Cleaning
30 Brookdale Road
Swords
Co. Dublin
☎ Dublin 8407515

Joe Walsh
Advance Cleaners
Pinewood Business Park
Whitemill Road
Wexford
☎ 053 45500

Ian and Judy Brooks
Image Contracts
Knocknacally
Youghal
Co. Cork
☎ 024 92984

First aid for minor accidents:

There will be some small accidents with which you may want to deal yourself, because in any normal household you will have spillages. The golden rule is to deal with all spillages as *quickly* as possible.

First, blot them up immediately and gently; never rub or scrub. Use plenty of blotting paper if you have it – *white* blotting paper – or clean, *undyed* absorbent cotton cloth, or *white* kitchen paper. Some spillages may contain dyes and liquids with an acid content, which can permanently alter the carpet dyes if not dealt with immediately.

If the carpet is very wet and and a large area is affected, lift it, if possible, off the floor so that air can circulate to speed up the drying process. If the underlay is stained, it also must be dried. You should never replace furniture or use the affected portion until it is completely dry.

For solid spillages use a blunt knife or spoon and work from the edge of the stain towards the centre. Sticky and beverage-type stains can generally be treated with a detergent solution, suitable for use on carpeting, and dry-cleaning solvents can be used on grease and oil stains. Carpets with a synthetic content or with foam backing or underlay can be adversely affected by some dry-cleaning solvents, so they must always be used with caution and care. Do a test area first.

In treating an expensive carpet, you should always proceed with caution. Blot up what you can blot up, remove what you can with a blunt knife if the spillage is solid, then check carefully before you apply any other treatment. You want to be sure that the treatment you are giving won't actually damage your carpet rather than remove the stain. If in any doubt, call in the professionals.

Different substances demand different treatments, and some substances are particularly aggressive: there is an orange dye in some fizzy drinks which is especially invasive and difficult to get out. There are, however, some treatments which are worth noting and which can be tried as an emergency measure.

Alcohol: Mix 30 ml of carpet shampoo or washing-up liquid with 5 ml (one teaspoonful) of white vinegar and 120 ml of water. Flush out the stain, blot with a thick wad of white toilet or kitchen paper, and repeat until the stain has gone.

Ball-point pen ink: Methylated spirits.

Beer: Mix 30 ml of carpet shampoo or washing-up liquid with 5 ml (one teaspoonful) of white vinegar and 120 ml of water. Flush out the stain, blot with a thick wad of white toilet or kitchen paper, and repeat until the stain has gone.

Blood: Cold water is essential. Tissue and iron, then use a mix of 30 ml of carpet shampoo or washing-up liquid with 5 ml (one teaspoonful) of white vinegar and 120 ml of water. Flush out the stain, blot with a thick wad of white toilet or kitchen paper, and repeat until the stain has gone.

Cellulose paint: Acetone.

Chewing gum: Perchlorethylene, commonly known as 'perk' – from your local chemist.

Coffee: Coffee can be a very difficult stain to remove. Try the mix of 30 ml of carpet shampoo or washing-up liquid with 5 ml (one teaspoonful) of white vinegar and 120 ml of water. Flush out the stain, blot with a thick wad of white toilet or kitchen paper, and keep repeating until the stain has gone. Finish with plain water with just a teaspoon of vinegar. Blot well. (And pray hard.)

Fat and oil: Tissue and iron, then use perchlorethylene. Do *not* use perk before ironing.

Grass: Methylated spirits.

Gravy: Perchlorethylene.

Ink: Water.

Jam: Lukewarm water with a drop of detergent.

Milk: Milk can be difficult because of the cream. Try mixing 30 ml of carpet shampoo or washing-up liquid with 5 ml (one teaspoonful) of white vinegar and 120 ml of water. Flush out the stain, blot with a thick wad of white toilet or kitchen paper, and repeat until the stain has gone.

Nail varnish: Acetone.

Salad cream: Use perchlorethylene, then mix 30 ml of carpet shampoo or washing-up liquid with 5 ml (one teaspoonful) of white vinegar and 120 ml of water. Flush out the stain, blot with a thick wad of white toilet or kitchen paper, and repeat until the stain has gone.

Shoe polish: Perchlorethylene.

Tar: Perchlorethylene.

Tea: Use water with a little detergent.

Urine: This stain must be removed as quickly as possible, as the chemicals in urine attack dyestuffs. Add a teaspoon of vinegar to 120 ml of water and a drop, no more than a drop, of Scrubb's ammonia. Flush out the stain, blot well and repeat until it has gone.

With **animal urine**, particularly tom-cat urine, it can be very difficult to get rid of the smell, which is particularly foul and all-pervasive. However, it *can* be eradicated, says **Ronnie Butler** of **Ideal Cleaning Services**. He has treated many carpets for just this problem, and his treatment works.

There is a minimum call-out charge, and in very bad cases it may be necessary to treat the underlay as well as the carpet, or even replace part of it if the damage has gone right through. You can contact Ronnie Butler at **Ideal Cleaning Services**, Monkstown Farm, Dun Laoghaire, Co. Dublin, ☎ Dublin 2801458.

Wine: Dilute carpet-shampoo solution, to which just a drop of ammonia has been added. Flush out, blot well and repeat as necessary.

You may, at some stage, feel that your whole carpet needs a good all-over clean. Ideally, you should get this done professionally, but there are a number of shampoos and cleaners available for DIY use. If you decide to do it yourself, it is imperative that the manufacturers' instructions are followed accurately, and a small portion of carpet, in an area normally covered by furniture, should be test cleaned before commencing the entire area.

You might also consider one of the 'wet-and-dry' vacuum cleaners now on the market which allow you to do your own carpet cleaning. They do quite an efficient job – but it's hard work. You need real energy in your elbows! Again, follow the instructions carefully.

If you are in any doubt at all, call in a professional cleaner. If you want just one stain removed, cleaners will do the job for you. Just remember that when you spot clean one part of a carpet, the rest of the carpet may look in need of cleaning as well.

Carpet pieces edged:

Many people have small pieces of good carpeting they would like to have edged to use as rugs or mats. **Eileen Lambert**, 52 South Avenue, Mount Merrion, Dublin, has made many people happy providing just that service. You can phone her at ☎ Dublin 2881555.

Scotchguarding:

This is a treatment which can be given to carpets to make them resistant to dirt and spillages, and which will render them easier to clean if accidents do happen. It is best done when a carpet is new; if not new the carpet should be clean and in good condition. Two firms who will Scotchguard your carpet are the following.

Ideal Cleaning Services Ltd
Monkstown Farm
Dun Laoghaire
Co. Dublin
☎ Dublin 2801458

Image Contracts
Knocknacally
Youghal
Co. Cork
☎ 024 92984

• cases (leather), repaired

'Bag Repairs'
Peter Cleary
11 Montague Lane
off Camden Street
Dublin 2

• cassette recorders

The Repair Centre, 46 Harrington Street, near Kelly's corner, Dublin, ☎ Dublin 757586, is run by a father and son, William and Brian Sweeney. There have been Sweeneys in Harrington Street for over thirty years. They repair cassette recorders and Walkmans and valve radios, as well as television sets, video recorders, car radios, stereo equipment and most small domestic appliances.

• cast iron

Oliver Harte, Knoxtown, Clonroche, Co. Wexford, ☎ 054 44110, does a lot of work in cast iron for local authorities as well as for private individuals. He will make railings, fire grates, gates, lamps – again it is much easier and cheaper if you can supply a pattern.

• cellos, repaired and restored

William Hofmann
(William Hofmann and Conchobhar Ruiseal)
Unit 1a
Greystones Shopping Centre
Delgany Road
Greystones, Co. Wicklow
☎ Dublin 2873299

Hugo Vegter (IPCRA)
Ivy Cottage
Glenmore, Cobh
Co. Cork
☎ 021 813352

• cement

Small quantities of cement, ready mixed and delivered to your door, are provided by **Mini Mix Concrete Ltd**, Ratoath, Co. Meath, ☎ Dublin 256323.

• ceramic (see china and ceramic, repaired and restored)

chimneys

Problems:

There are common chimney problems and common misconceptions about chimneys. People quite regularly complain that there is a 'down-draught' on their chimney. In fact, people often confuse a down-draught with inadequate up-draught. Down-draught only occurs when the wind comes from a certain direction, so it only happens from time to time – not every day. If your problem can be clearly defined as a down-draught, then the answer is to build your chimney higher – above the level of whatever is causing the down-draught, which could be another part of the house or an adjacent building.

Inadequate up-draught can be a fairly constant problem and not just something that happens when the wind is blowing from a particular quarter. It could be caused by one of several things. If you have a large fireplace, and a chimney that is too narrow in diameter to suit it, then you can get inadequate up-draught. If your windows and doors are so well sealed that there is inadequate air combustion getting through to your fire, then you can get inadequate up-draught, and this is a problem which has occurred in recent years with increased insulation. To conserve heat, for example, more and more people – quite properly – insulated their attic spaces and installed double glazing, draught sealed windows which weren't double glazed, and draught proofed doors.

However, a fire needs a supply of air in order to burn properly. If insulation is done so well that all sources of air are closed off, a chimney which never smoked before can suddenly start smoking. You need air in your room for two reasons: one, to serve your chimney, and two, because you must have one-and-a-half air changes an hour in a room, otherwise you will get drowsy and feel out of sorts. One answer is to install a Draughtmaster, which is a gadget that can be put in over the door leading into your room. It pulls in the air from a high level so that there are no draughts, and it is stabilised to release the right amount of air at the right time. It should be generally available in good hardware shops and builders' providers.

If the construction of your chimney is faulty so that smoke gets trapped on the way up, then you can also get inadequate up-draught. Quite frequently, you will hear people saying that a black, tar-like substance is coming down their chimney, usually the chimney of a solid-fuel cooker. The two most likely causes for this state of affairs are damp fuel and a cold, unlined chimney. In this country we tend to be rather careless about what we burn in our solid-fuel appliances. Not infrequently we burn damp turf, unseasoned wood and even the kitchen rubbish. Turf must be dry. Wood must be dry and seasoned – on the continent they keep wood for two years and sometimes for three years before they regard it as being fit to burn.

Here in Ireland we not infrequently saw up a fallen tree and put the logs straight into the fire. Equally, your kitchen rubbish can be a mass of damp vegetable peelings or some other similarly sodden mixture. All this moisture has to go somewhere, and what happens is a bit like what happens when you get condensation on your windows on a cold day – the moisture goes up to condense with the combusted products on the inside of the chimney. This is particularly likely if your chimney is a cold one. Hot flue gases rise, meet the cold chimney, and condense and run down again, bringing all the old soot and tar along with them.

The ideal chimney goes through the middle of a house and therefore is protected from wind and weather for a good part of its length. If it's constructed in brick, then it's likely to be warm. But if it's on a gable wall or freestanding on a boiler house apart from the main house, then it's more likely to be a cold chimney. If you have a masonry chimney on an outer wall of the house, it is recommended that you insulate the liner with a suitable material – a vermiculite mix. Your local hardware shop should be able to supply you with the materials.

Remember that all chimneys must be kept clean, and it is recommended that you have them swept twice during the heating season.

Chimney specialists:

Joe Manifold is an absolute wealth of information on everything to do with chimneys, both for solid-fuel and for gas appliances. If you have a problem with your chimney, he will be able to solve it; if you are planning to build a chimney, it could be a very good idea to call him in before you start. Building a good and proper chimney requires particular skills, knowledge and expertise. A badly built chimney can be inefficient and smokey, and it can also be very dangerous. Over the years Joe has examined thousands and thousands of chimneys, and he says quite a remarkable number of them were faulty in some way. You'll find **Joe Manifold** at 40 Sundrive Road, Kimmage, Dublin, ☎ Dublin 967355.

You can also get advice on fireplaces and chimneys from the Byrne family of **Bells Fireplaces**, 122 Botanic Road, Glasnevin, Dublin, ☎ Dublin 301777. They have been making fireplaces and peering up chimneys since 1939.

You might also contact **Jimmy Rushe**, 12 Kennellsfort Road Lower, Palmerstown, Dublin 20, ☎ Dublin 6262229, who has much experience of chimneys and their problems.

Chimney and boiler cleaning:

Kevin Ward
Domestic Cleaning Services
153 Glenmaroon Road
Palmerstown
Dublin 20
☎ Dublin 6268217

• china and ceramic, repaired and restored

Most people have a special piece of china or porcelain which they've bought, been given or inherited – it may have only sentimental value, or it may be worth a considerable amount. Very often, it's the piece which you most care about that gets damaged. Some pieces can be repaired relatively easily, others may take a professional restorer weeks of work in research, in slowly building up a missing fragment, and in finishing and painting until the repair is completely invisible to any but the most experienced and knowledgeable eye.

If you have a piece which has been broken and which you would like to have mended, there are various people to whom you can bring it. Desiree Shortt in 38 North Great George's Street, Dublin, is the *doyenne* of china and porcelain restoration. She has been restoring for almost twenty years and has trained many people who are now working in this field all over Ireland, and in many other parts of the world as well.

Fitzmaurice China Restoration
Shandon Craft Centre
Shandon Street
Cork
☎ 021 395317

The Glebe Studios (IPCRA)
Straffan
Co. Kildare
☎ Dublin 6271129

Leinster Studios (IPCRA)
Eileen O'Leary and Anne Reeves-Smyth
10 Leinster Square
Rathmines
Dublin 6
☎ Dublin 974009

Desiree Shortt (IPCRA)
38 North Great George's Street
Dublin 6
☎ Dublin 722285

Ray Simmons (IPCRA)
37 Montpelier Parade
Monkstown Road
Co. Dublin
☎ Dublin 2842038

Jenny Slevin (IPCRA)
19 Longford Terrace
Monkstown
Co. Dublin
☎ Dublin 2803429

• clairol hair care

Gavins Shaver Centre
83 Lower Camden Street
Dublin 2
☎ Dublin 757109
(*Republic of Ireland*)

Domestic Sales and Repair Services
219 Kingsway
Dunmurry
Belfast BT17 9SB
☎ 0232 301533
(Northern Ireland)

cleaning

People call in house cleaners because they are having a party, because visitors are coming, because both husband and wife are out working and don't have time to do a really good spring clean, because they have a house which has been rented out to tenants who have left it in a mess, or simply to get somebody else to do a job they don't like doing themselves.

If you plan to get somebody in to do a clean-up, make a list telling them *precisely* what you want them to do. Do you want the cooker cleaned? If it is very dirty, then this could take one member of the team the best part of a morning. Do you want your windows washed? Your walls washed? Specify on your list. Do you want your carpets and upholstery cleaned? (Mary Nolan does, Mini Maids don't.) If you have everything down in black and white, it makes it easier for the cleaners and better value for yourself – you won't waste precious time trying to decide what you want them to do and in what order of priority.

Mary Nolan
Associated Cleaning Services
206 Springdale Road
Dublin 5
☎ Dublin 8478852

Mini Maids
6 Windsor Terrace
Church Road
Malahide
Co. Dublin
☎ Dublin 8452017

Mary Nolan has been in the business of cleaning houses, offices, schools and a variety of other buildings for twenty years. She has a wide range of equipment and staff who are not easily daunted by dirt – though they could tell some horrific stories. Mini Maids has been run by Noel Colville for some five years, but it has been in existence for almost ten. Both of them operate with cleaning teams, bringing their own materials and gear with them and charging by the hour.

In Cork **Ian** and **Judy Brooks** give an excellent service. They operate under the name of **Image Contracts**, and you'll find them at Knocknacally, Youghal, Co. Cork, ☎ 024 92984. They will clean your house inside and out, including the upholstery, the carpets, the windows and even pebble-dashed walls.

clocks

Knollys Stokes has always loved clocks. Older Cork people and visitors to Cork in days gone by – in fact, anybody who frequented the Old Bridge restaurant just beside Patrick's Bridge – will remember his collection of clocks. All his life he has been fascinated by them and remains so – he was one of the founding members of the Horology Society of Ireland. Though he never served a formal apprenticeship, his knowledge of clocks and their workings is quite unique.

Knollys' son Christopher grew up surrounded by clocks, and he opened Stokes Clock Shop some fifteen years ago. When Christopher's son Philip grew up he went to the Irish-Swiss School of Horology in Blanchardstown, Dublin, where he learned all about repairing watches, Swiss makes in particular. Today Christopher and his wife, Sally, with Philip, run the family business in MacCurtain Street, Cork. It is full of clocks of all sizes: big, small, middle-sized, very old and not quite so old, grandfather clocks, carriage clocks and mantelpiece clocks, all in various stages of repair.

The Stokes also *make* clocks – on a grand scale. For Dublin, they made the clock in the St Stephen's Green Centre, which is certainly the clock with the biggest face in Ireland and, they think, possibly in Europe. They also crafted the clock for the Royal Hibernian Way, and this clock gives the phases of the moon, 'Because there used to be a hotel where the shops are now, and in the old days phases of the moon were important to travellers. Bright nights were very important; in fact, if you look up the date of society functions in old times you will find that many were held on nights of a full moon. It made travelling easier.'

They restored the clock in Kilkenny's city hall after the building suffered seriously in a fire. There were four faces on the clock, all in cast iron, and the cast iron had become twisted in the fire. 'So we took them down and with the good bits made up a mould and cast for new faces. There was an electric motor in it when it was destroyed – this had been put into it quite a number of years before. But when we were restoring it, they decided in Kilkenny that they wanted to have everything absolutely correct, so we acquired an old manual movement out of a church which was closing and put that in.' You'll find the Stokeses at the following address.

Stokes Clock Shop
48 MacCurtain Street
Cork
☎ 021 509125

Antique clocks repaired:

People come from all over Ireland, and even from outside Ireland, bringing their clocks to **Pat Healy** for repair. Some clocks are valuable, he says, but many are not. 'But a clock can have enormous value for the person who owns it. Perhaps it belonged to a father or a grandfather. It may be special because somebody got it for a wedding or an anniversary present. Now it has stopped and they want to have it repaired. You've no idea how rewarding it is to give a clock back to someone like that, all polished and in good working order.' He does all the restoration with dedicated care and has worked with clocks for over twenty-five years.

Pat makes one heartfelt plea: if you have a genuine antique clock and are thinking of having a quartz movement fitted, please think again. Virtually all antique clocks can be repaired, he says, and to fit a quartz movement in a genuine antique clock is a positive crime – apart from the fact that it hugely diminishes its value. You'll find Pat and Marie Healy at the address below.

The Clock Centre
71 York Road
Dun Laoghaire
Co. Dublin
☎ Dublin 2803667

Anne Reeves-Smyth of **Leinster Studios** (IPCRA) specialises in the restoration of clock *faces*. You can contact her at Leinster Studios, 10 Leinster Square, Rathmines, Dublin 6, ☎ Dublin 974009.

Clocks are also repaired by the following shops.

Timepiece Antiques
58 Patrick Street
Dublin
☎ Dublin 540774

Ken Homan
91 Sorrento Road
Dalkey
Co. Dublin
☎ Dublin 2858364

Mark Causer
22b Magazine Road
Cork
☎ 021 311463

Robert Barfoot (IPCRA)
9 York Parade
Belfast BT15 3QZ
☎ 0232 773108

Quartz movements fitted:

You may have a clock which has been part of family life for as long as you can remember but is not working any more. It may not be a very valuable or good-looking piece, but you hope to have it in working order again. Edmund Ryan fits quartz movements into clocks like this. You will find **Edmund Ryan** at 67 Monastery Drive, Clondalkin, Co. Dublin, ☎ Dublin 591432.

• colston appliances

Derrick Cox
30 Meadow Vale
Blackrock
Co. Dublin
☎ Dublin 2895580
(*Republic of Ireland*)

Merloni Domestic Appliances Ltd
35 Little Donegal Street
Belfast BT1 2JD
☎ 0232 242420
(*Northern Ireland*)

condensation

Condensation is quite a problem in many houses for a number of different reasons. The potential for condensation exists wherever people live and wherever moisture is produced. Moisture arises in steam from cooking and washing, from bathing and showering, from clothes which are being dried, and from gas cooking and gas- and oil-fuelled heating. When you breathe on a mirror and it fogs up, that's condensation.

Condensation has always been with us, but over the last ten years its impact has been much more pronounced. When the price of oil and heating fuels went up, people cut down on their heating, increased insulation and draught sealed their windows and doors – all of which is recommended. But while insulation is desirable, so is adequate ventilation. In some cases, people draught sealed and insulated their houses so well that they ended up without sufficient ventilation. If there is no heat to help evaporate moisture, if there is no ventilation to allow it to escape outside, then moisture will appear on the nearest cold surface. Very often this can be the north-facing wall of a bedroom or an extension, the kind commonly built on to the back of a house with two or three outside walls and perhaps a flat roof. The obvious areas where you can expect to find condensation are in kitchens and bathrooms.

Cooking and washing in a kitchen will naturally cause condensation. Extractor fans help to a degree, but what you have to do is try to control the amount of steam being produced. When pots come to the boil, turn them down. When you are doing a lot of cooking, open a window if things begin to get steamed up. Use an automatic electric kettle rather than one which has to be manually switched off or taken off the hob – this will save fuel costs as well.

You can do a considerable amount to cut down on condensation in the bathroom. Put the cold water into the bath before the hot water is turned on. People don't always like doing this, particularly if they have a cast-iron enamel bath; when they get into it the base of the bath may feel a bit chilly on their bottoms – however, putting in the cold water first definitely does cut down on condensation. Install a suitable wall heater in your bathroom and make sure you open the window when you get out of the bath. Try to strike a balance between heat and ventilation.

There are other reasons for an increase in condensation. Many houses are now unoccupied during the day because both husband and wife are out working, so the house is unheated and unventilated for considerable periods of time. This can also mean that a household does its cooking and cleaning in the evenings or weekends, producing large quantities of moisture over short periods of time. The reduction in the number of open fireplaces in houses has also decreased ventilation.

Everybody is familiar with the unpleasant effects of condensation, from water streaming down walls, to ugly mould growths, to pools of water on the inside window sills. Mould growth on walls is caused by airborne spores deposited on walls by atmospheric moisture during condensation. You'll find mould growing on walls, in corners, under windows, and generally in areas where air movement is restricted. In severe cases it can spoil curtains, carpets and bedding.

There is no one simple answer to condensation. Striking a compromise is what it's all about, really. In the days of cheap oil, people with oil-fired central heating who saw condensation on their walls simply turned up the heating and opened the windows. But the days of really cheap oil are gone, and having done as much as we can to control the obvious sources of condensation, the next thing to do is to strike a compromise between the heat you can afford and the necessary ventilation to go with it.

If you have cold walls in rooms other than a kitchen or a bathroom, you might like to consider the benefits of dry-lining. This is commonly done with polystyrene slabs wedged between timber battens, and the whole sheeted with wallboard. It can make a considerable difference in a previously cold room. Condensation shouldn't occur in good double-glazed windows, but it can be a problem with single-glazed ones. Again, ventilation is important. One person sleeping in a room at night can cause quite a degree of condensation on a window and two people even more. Some ventilation is essential.

You should also be sure that your curtains are hung well clear of your windows because if there *is* any condensation, and your curtains are against the window, the lining will end up with mildew spots, which are very unsightly and virtually impossible to remove without damage. The same is true of blinds. Blinds should not be too near the window, and they should be hung well free of the window bottom, because if condensation has gathered there, then the blinds will also become mildewed.

There is no easy answer to condensation because there is no one cause. The solution is in recognising the different causes and doing your best to control them. For advice on methods and products which control condensation, go to **The Damp Store**, 20 Store Street, Dublin 1, ☎ Dublin 745055.

• consumer complaints

The Consumer Personal Service was set up to assist consumers in obtaining fair play and justice from retailers and service providers, where valid complaints are concerned. The association is prepared to pursue certain cases all the way to court, if necessary, when important matters of principle affecting all consumers are raised. There is a small charge, slightly more for non-members of the Consumer Service than for members. The association welcomes new members, and the more members the association has the stronger it is. If you want to find out more about the **Consumer Personal Service,** telephone ☎ Dublin 612293. If you want to take out a subscription to *Consumer Choice* and become a member of the association, write to the subscription department at 45 Upper Mount Street, Dublin 2, ☎ Dublin 686836. There is also an advice and information service, for members only, which can be reached at ☎ Dublin 612466.

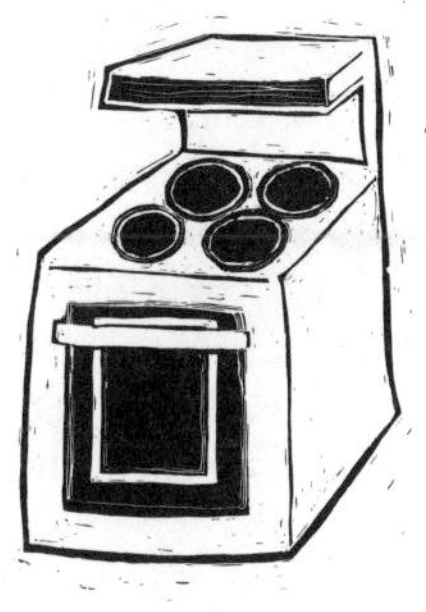

cookers

Parts for Stanley solid-fuel cookers:

Cliffords
Gardiner Lane
Dublin 1
☎ Dublin 746457

To buy:

There are a variety of electric ovens available for today's cooks. There is the conventional oven, with the traditional top and bottom heat, which is probably best for cooking roast meat or for baking bread. There is the fan oven, which gives almost the same heat throughout the oven – the emphasis is on the 'almost', because fan ovens don't give perfectly unified heat. In general, however, you can use two or three shelves in the oven at the same time so that you can batch bake – trays of scones and biscuits and a cake with either. The fan oven is particularly good for sponges and cakes and for cooking different foods together without blurring flavour. You can, for instance, cook fish and a pudding at the same time – the flavours won't mingle.

Then there is the multi-function oven, which can be used as a fan oven or as a conventional oven, and which may have, in some cases, a turbo-grill facility – this means you can grill and use the fan oven simultaneously: excellent for oven-fried chicken.

Over the years, oven design and oven fashions have changed. Eight or nine years ago, people usually bought a double oven. The idea was that you used the big oven for big occasions and the smaller oven for everyday use – for quick meals or when you were just cooking for two or three people. In practice, many people found they didn't need two ovens. Nowadays, with microwave ovens a commonplace in most homes, people are opting more and more for the single oven. A sensible choice might be a single oven and a combination microwave oven, which works both as a small oven and as a microwave. You can even get one which incorporates a grill as well. This way you can get the best of both worlds.

The size of an oven is very important. The usual criteria in Ireland is that an oven should be big enough to cook the Christmas turkey in. So when you go out to buy, look carefully at the size of the oven and make sure you buy one suitable for the kind of cooking you do. It's also a good idea to look at the venting on any oven you buy and get one with as few vents as possible – vents are fiddly to clean. Look at the door: it should be of good, heavy quality. Ask if a drip pan comes with the oven; it can be very useful. Look for good edges and a good finish. Try, if you can, to get an oven with glass over the control panel, otherwise the lettering tends to wear off.

Ovens can get dirty and are difficult to clean if not done on a regular basis. You might consider a self-cleaning oven or an oven with catalytic liners. Self-cleaning ovens are better than ovens with catalytic liners because the catalytic liners are not usually self-cleaning in the long term. We do a lot of roasting in Ireland and the good goes out of the liners in about five years. If you *do* buy an oven with catalytic liners, make sure you can replace the liners – some you can take out and replace, some you can't.

A useful tip: if you already have catalytic liners and are finding them hard to clean, look up a friend with a self-cleaning oven. If the liners are placed in a self-cleaning oven, the oven will clean them. These ovens work by raising the temperature of the empty oven to 260°C (500°F) so that any soiling is completely carbonised, and you can just wipe it out – a catalyser neutralises the products of carbonisation to prevent impure air being discharged. During the process a tamper-proof door lock guards against accidental openings of the door during the cleaning cycle. The whole process takes between thirty and ninety minutes, depending on the degree of soil. And it really works very well indeed – the perfect answer for all those people, including this writer, who hate cleaning ovens. It should be said, however, that ovens with this kind of facility are at the top end of the market and don't come cheap.

Natural gas can be a wonderful way to cook, and liquid petroleum gas is also an excellent cooking fuel. The range of gas cookers on the market is also improving (and there was room for improvement).

Every household needs a grill. You can have a separate grill or you can grill in your oven. A separate grill is a much better idea. When you are looking at a separate grill, don't just ask for a grill, ask for a variable grill with different settings and not just an on-and-off switch. If you are having it built in, think about where you are going to put it. You don't want it so low that a small child can reach it – most grills work with the door open – but neither do you want it on top of your oven, because then the steam and cooking deposits from the grill will rise to the unit directly above. It's better to put your grill under your oven, then any dirt that goes up will clean easily off your oven door.

Finally, when you are buying a grill, be sure you get one that includes the grill pan, the mesh and the handle – surprisingly, not all grills automatically come with these vital pieces.

Cooker hobs:

Every kitchen has to have a cooking hob. This can be solid fuel, gas or electric. Gas is traditionally the choice of dedicated cooks. If you're buying one, go for one that doesn't have too many bits and pieces; this means too much cleaning.

When it comes to electric hobs, you can choose between a ceramic hob or a hob with solid plates. Ceramic hobs are much easier to clean than the latter – you only have one flat surface. They are also more convenient to use than traditional-style hobs; you can move saucepans around easily on a flat surface and they are better than solid plates, which can take too long to heat up and too long to cool down. But a certain amount of care is needed in using a ceramic hob. If you drop something on it, it *could* break. So, if yours is a house where a lot of people are going to be using the cooker, and where it may not get the care it needs, you might be better off with a hob with solid plates.

What kind of things get dropped on a ceramic hob? Obviously, one item that comes to mind is a heavy saucepan; if a cast-iron saucepan, for example, slips from your hands down on the hob, then there's a good chance you will break it. But ceramic hobs have also been broken by things falling from shelves above the cooker, like spice jars. If you do have a ceramic hob it might be worth considering getting insurance coverage in your household policy against breakage. The annual cost is minimal and it could make a big difference if you find yourself having to replace the hob.

The usual recommendation is that ceramic hob cleaners and green nylon pads are best for cleaning hobs, though a scraper is also provided with most of them. Personally, as somebody who enjoys using a ceramic hob, I have no compunction about using a scraper. When I lost the one I was given, I simply bought one of the little Stanley tools for scraping paint off windows, available in most hardware stores. But if you are a fanatic about having a hob with an unmarked appearance, perhaps you shouldn't use the scraper because it could on occasions leave tiny scratch marks.

One of the criticisms of electricity has always been that you cannot control the heat as easily as you can with gas – that the rings don't heat up as quickly and that you can't reduce the heat immediately when you want to do so. Electric hobs have improved enormously over the years, and with the advent of the halogen hob, we were told that we were getting very much improved control. Undoubtedly, control generally has improved, but it is arguable whether halogen rings are worth the extra money you pay for them. Yes, they do heat up a bit faster, but do you really *need* to have your plates heat up so quickly? And are you prepared to pay considerably more to have that extra bit of heat?

Some hobs have just one halogen ring. If you have only one on your hob the chances are you'll use it all the time, because you see it lighting up quickly. Eventually, you will overuse it and it will get burnt out.

If you would like to use both gas *and* electricity, you can buy a domino hob, which is a hob with two gas and two electric rings. You can get a combination of two gas rings with two solid-plate electric rings, or two rings in a ceramic hob. This kind of combination, however, can be quite expensive. If money is no object, you could have two electric rings on a ceramic hob, two gas rings, and a built-in deep-fat fryer *or* barbecue *or* gas wok.

Whichever hob you decide to buy, try to get one with the smaller plate or plates in the front and the larger ones at the back. If you can, get one with the control panel at the side, separated from the actual hob by a guard and preferably covered with glass. It will be much easier to keep clean.

Cooker hoods:

Every kitchen is going to produce a considerable quantity of steam, cooking smells and grease. If you don't make provision for getting these out of the kitchen as they are produced, your walls and your ceiling will suffer.

If you are planning a new kitchen or about to buy a cooker hood for an existing kitchen, it's important that you give the matter careful thought. To enable your cooker hood to do its job with maximum efficiency, the best place to have your cooker and hood is against an outside wall. This means that after the grease is caught by the filter, the steam and the smells can get directly outside in the minimum of time. Even if your cooker is on an inside wall, it may still be possible to duct it to an outside wall. Modern kitchen units rarely go up to ceiling level, so ducting can be carried from the cooker along the top of the units and still be invisible. The maximum length of ducting recommended with an ordinary cooker hood is ten feet. If you have to duct further, you will have to think in terms of a stronger fan than the one commonly found on domestic hoods. The longer the ducting the stronger the fan must be.

There are various brands of cooker hoods, but nearly all have a fan for extracting and a filter to trap dirt and grease. This filter can be a washable filter, a disposable filter, or a charcoal or carbon filter. The filters must be properly maintained, which means they must be kept clean, and they must be changed when necessary.

When you are considering what kind of cooker hood and extraction system to buy, you should also consider the area it is going to serve. You must take into account the width of your hob and the equipment on it. Some modern kitchens have domino units with a choice of gas or electric rings. Some may even have a built-in deep-fat fryer. Many people have a free-standing deep-fat fryer, and a deep-fat fryer produces a very considerable amount of oily steam. If you use a deep-fat fryer a lot, you might like to consider getting a cooker hood which will not only cover your hob but also an area beside it so that you can use your deep-fat fryer underneath and get rid of all the steam.

Cooker hoods must always be installed twenty-four to thirty-two inches above the cooking surface. On conventional cookers this means the hob. On cookers with eye-level grills, this must be sixty-one to eighty-one centimetres above the grill surface, and there are some kitchen fitters who won't install a cooker hood over a hob with an eye-level grill.

The outside vents for your fan should not be ordinary building vents, but vents specifically designed for an extractor fan, fitted with a non-return flap so that the wind doesn't blow back. If you are going to have a built-in barbecue, then you will need a down-draughted extractor fan, vented out through the wall behind it.

Like other appliances, an extractor hood can be integrated into your kitchen, again providing it is a suitable hood. You can have it under a canopy hood – for example, a copper canopy. The latest hood is the telescopic hood, which is very slimlined indeed – only about two-and-a-half centimetres in depth.

Don't expect a cooker hood and a fan to work miracles. They will remove most of the steam and smoke, but shouldn't be expected to remove it all instantly. A lot will depend on the size of your room, the width of your hob, the equipment you are using and how much you are using at a time. It is also recommended that you leave the hood turned on for up to twenty minutes after you finish cooking.

Repairs:

If you have a problem with your cooker, you'll find the service agent listed alphabetically under the cooker's brand name.

• creda cookers and hobs

Ideal Service Ltd
Kylemore Park West
Ballyfermot
Dublin 10
☎ Dublin 6266720

Parts only:

Charlie Shiels
Golden Bridge Industrial Estate
Inchicore
Dublin 8
☎ Dublin 545844
(Republic of Ireland)

Creda Care
256 Ormeau Road
Belfast BT7 2FZ
☎ 0232 641401
(Northern Ireland)

Refrigerators:

Hotpoint Service
256 Ormeau Road
Belfast BT7 2FZ
☎ 0232 647111

• crystal repairs

A. C. Taylor
Upper Sandwith Street
Dublin 2
☎ Dublin 765441

• curtain cleaning

Most good dry cleaners will clean curtains. It may be even better to have the cleaners come to your house, take down your curtains, clean them, and come back and rehang them. **Crown Cleaners** offer this service for a small additional charge, which many people feel is well worth paying. You'll find them at the following addresses.

Crown Cleaners
81 Lower Camden Street
Dublin 8
☎ Dublin 753584/782407

7 Fitzmorris Road
Dublin 11
☎ Dublin 343914

91 Cabra Road
Dublin 7
☎ Dublin 300257

Greenhills Arcade
Jamestown Road
Dublin 12
☎ Dublin 507663

damp

Damp can manifest itself in a variety of ways, and dealing with damp can be very frustrating. Before you begin to try to address the problem you have to identify the cause, and this can often be the biggest difficulty of all. Diagnoses differ and the damp can go on.

There are many reasons for dampness, but the main causes are rising damp, leakage from pipes or drains, rain penetration and condensation. A number of common sources of rising damp have their origin in a faulty or non-existent damp-proof course. Rising damp is a frequent problem in both old and new buildings. In older buildings the problem is usually due to the fact that no damp-proof course exists. In new buildings the problem is usually associated with improperly placed damp-proof courses.

The absence or failure of a damp-proof course in walls usually produces efflorescence from ground salts, which eventually causes decay and damage to internal plaster. Hygroscopic salts tend to retain moisture, leaving the plaster permanently wet, and these salts also have the ability to draw moisture from the atmosphere. Naturally, skirtings, timber frames and other fittings in the room also become affected – with the added possibility of wet or even dry rot.

Other common problem sources are the failure to fit damp-proof coursing properly around window sills, the omission of weep holes above damp-proof courses, the incorrect positioning of the external edge of a damp-proof course in relation to window frames, and old damp-proof course materials which may have broken up.

It cannot be emphasised too strongly that damp-proof courses are a very important part of the building fabric of a house, and they need to be very carefully installed with good workmanship by the craftsmen and careful supervision by the contractor.

Leaking pipes, a frequent contributor to dampness, can come in many forms, and a faulty leak is difficult to solve, particularly if it happens to be far from the visible signs of dampness. Defective gutter pipes with bad joins and clogged gutter pipes, from which leaves and debris are not removed, can act as a bridge, causing a build-up of moisture on the wall surfaces which may eventually cause damp patches internally.

If you have a defective downpipe with bad joins, instead of flowing down, rainwater from the gutter will escape into the wall. If the gutter running below your roof is jammed with moss and grit, the water will overflow during heavy rain and soak down into the walls and woodwork. Care should always be taken to ensure that pipes do not touch the external surface of the wall. Leaks in gutters are not always readily detected, and considerable damage may be done before they become evident.

A split window sill may seem a small fault, but it can let water soak into a large area of wall beneath it. Rain penetration sounds an easy one to identify, but sometimes it is and sometimes it isn't. A tile has slipped, a slate has cracked or broken. A gutter may be blocked, and in bad weather the water finds the easiest course – very often into the wrong place: your home. Sometimes you may only become aware of the trouble when the water has been leaking in for quite a while. And even then, locating the source may be a more difficult matter. The leak through your roof, for instance, may not be over the actual point where it shows up on your ceiling, but from a broken tile much higher up and some distance away. A faulty flat roof can allow rain in; a defect in the window frame and surround can cause trouble.

Rain can also affect the walls of your house, through faulty wall surfaces and damaged pointing. These particular areas are tricky to identify and treat. Hollow block walls, for example, built from one single line of twenty-three-centimetre hollow blocks, are to be found in very many houses all over the country; this is, perhaps, the most commonly found form of wall construction. A hollow block wall depends almost entirely on the externally applied finish for its weather proofness. If this finish cracks, if it is faulty, or if it isn't put on properly – and builders are not above skimping on both the mix and the number of coats – after a number of years rain can begin to penetrate the finish and eventually get through to the internal walls, which is usually the point at which the average householder first becomes aware of the problem.

A cavity wall, as the names suggests, is made up of two walls with a cavity in between them, and one of the objects of the cavity is to prevent moisture from the outer wall getting through to the second inner wall. This usually works quite well, but problems can occur when the two walls are connected by wall ties, or around openings. Certain forms of internal wall insulation can also cause problems if the walls have not been carefully constructed in the first place, and if the insulation isn't properly done. The kind of internal wall insulation which is injected into the cavity should always be performed by a reputable and reliable firm, and the walls themselves should be carefully checked beforehand to make sure they are suitable for such insulation.

If you live in a brick house, and the mortar joint between the bricks has begun to crumble, it should be repaired not only for the sake of appearance, but to keep rain out of the wall. Rain alone is bad for a house, but the real danger is rain followed by frost, because if water soaks into the bricks and then freezes and expands, the surface of the bricks can crack. Repointing the mortar when it begins to go will be much cheaper than dealing with cracked and damaged bricks.

Water can seep through your walls at a lower level if you've been careless about the outside ground. A flower bed, up against the wall of a house, may slowly build up above the damp-course level without your being aware of it. And the rain and surface water can accumulate and get through. Accumulated debris, autumn leaves, a path around the house on which the level has gradually built up over the years as more gravel is added, mixing with the subsoil so that the all-over level rises above the damp-course – all of these things can bring damp into your house.

A dehumidifier can be very effective in dealing with the immediate problems of damp or condensation. You can buy one or hire one by the day or week. However, it's worth remembering that a dehumidifier deals with the results of damp or condensation, not with the causes. It is an excellent quick solution until you can deal with the problem properly.

For advice on methods and products for controlling damp, go to **The Damp Store**, 20 Store Street, Dublin 1, ☎ Dublin 745055.

• de dietrich hobs and cookers

F. E. Smith Electrical Ltd
3/5 Camden Place
Dublin 2
☎ Dublin 751702

• de longhi appliances

Electroservice
Long Mile Road
Dublin 12
☎ Dublin 518666

• delmore appliances

Kitchen Appliance Distributors
Unit 13, Cherry Orchard Industrial Estate
Dublin 10
☎ Dublin 6266798

• dimplex

Dimpco Ltd
Airport Road
Cloghran
Dublin 9
☎ Dublin 8428222

In Northern Ireland contact Brownbrook Distributors for the name of your nearest service person.

Brownbrook Distributors Ltd
Unit 24, Seagoe Industrial Estate
Portadown
Co. Armagh BT63 5TH
☎ 0762 337317

• disabled, services for the (see handicapped)

dishwashers

Dishwashers are not as common as washing machines in Irish homes, but they should be, because washing dishes is a dirty, repetitive, boring job. You don't need a dishwasher with an elaborate number of programmes, nor are quick programmes a great advantage – generally they don't wash the dishes properly. You *do* need to wash at 50°C or 60°C to get a decent wash. Check how much water the machine uses – that is, how many litres. The more water it uses, the more you have to heat.

Check the noise level. Some machines have quite a high decibel level, and some are as quiet as forty-eight decibels. Inspect the door: if it's good and strong the noise will be less; if it's integrated, it will be even lower. Does the dishwasher take twelve-inch (thirty-centimetre) dinner plates? You must be able to fit a good-sized dinner plate in your machine, and not all machines take them happily. Check to see if it has an anti-flooding device, which will turn off the water if the machine breaks down. Finally, remember that if you live in an apartment, and if space is at a premium, you can now get small dishwashers for small spaces.

Repairs:

If you have a problem with your dishwasher, you'll find the service agent listed alphabetically under the dishwasher's brand name.

• dolls

If you have members of your family who like dolls, you should visit **The Doll Store and Doll's Hospital** in Lower George's Street, Dublin. As well as making dolls' houses and miniature furniture, **Melissa Nolan**, who runs the shop, has a big selection of dolls she has crafted herself – reproduction, turn-of-the-century French dolls. She also stocks dolls from about six other good Irish doll makers and repairs and restores.

The Doll Store and Doll's Hospital
62 South Great
George's Street
Dublin 2
☎ Dublin 783403

• dometec appliances

Bluebell Appliance Service Ltd
Naas Road
Dublin 12
☎ Dublin 783955/508455

• double basses, repaired and restored (see viols)

• dreamland electric blankets

Appliance Network Services Ltd
19 East Essex Street
Dublin 2
☎ Dublin 6795244/715528

In Northern Ireland, send blankets back to England.

Dreamland Appliances Ltd
Vine Mill
Royton
Oldham OL2 5LN
☎ 061 6521211

• drawings, repaired and restored

Susan Corr (IPCRA)
Paper Conservation Studio
48 Woodley Park
Dundrum
Dublin
☎ Dublin 2987661

Pat McBride (IPCRA)
Paper Conservation Studio
IDA Tower Complex
Pearse Street
Dublin 2
☎ Dublin 775655

David Skinner (IPCRA)
Paper Conservation Studio
Celbridge Mill
Celbridge
Co. Kildare
☎ Dublin 6272913

• duvet cleaning

The Kelso Laundry
Rathmines Road
Dublin 6
☎ Dublin 972089/978490

Celtic Linen Services
St Magdalens
Wexford
☎ 053 422244

In Northern Ireland contact the following services.

Erne Laundry Ltd
Henry Street
Enniskillen BT74 7JX
☎ 0365 322137

Lilliput (Dunmurry) Ltd
Glenburn Road
Dunmurry
Belfast BT17 9AP
☎ 0232 618555

Standard Laundry (Northern Ireland) Ltd
213/215 Donegall Avenue
Belfast BT12 6LU
☎ 0232 327295

Waveney Laundry Ltd
Clonavon
Ballymena BT43 5BJ
☎ 0266 42131

Repairs, alterations and additions:

The Quiltcare Centre
Grantham House
Grantham Street
off Camden Street
Dublin 2
☎ Dublin 783922

easter eggs

Anybody who enjoys making their own Easter eggs might like to know that they will find egg moulds in **Kitchen Complements**, Chatham House, Chatham Street, Dublin 2, ☎ Dublin 770734. Kitchen Complements have quite a varied selection, including some excellent Irish-made moulds. If you live outside Dublin and want a mould or moulds posted to you, they'll be happy to oblige.

If you live in the Cork area, you might like to visit the **Ballymaloe Shop**, which is very much part of the good food scene on the Ballymaloe estate in Midleton, Co. Cork. They stock Easter egg moulds, among many other useful and delectable things. Wendy Allen runs it, and you can ring her at ☎ 021 652032.

elderly, care for the

Everybody likes their independence, and for many elderly people independence is something they particularly value. Few people like to admit that they can't cope on their own, but unfortunately, as people grow older and frailer they are more at risk of incurring accidents or sudden illnesses. Sons and daughters may feel that a parent will be safer living with them or in some sort of sheltered accommodation. However, a parent may feel very distressed at the thought of leaving a home in which they have spent most of their lives and where all their memories lie. There are various ways of tackling the problems involved.

One way is for an elderly person to join one of the care services which enables people living alone to contact a care centre manned by qualified staff at any time of the day or night. Pressing a button carried on his or her person will activate a request for help. The caller is automatically identified to the trained staff on duty, and full personal details come up on a visual display unit – these will have already been supplied by the user. The staff at the centre will be able to talk to the caller by means of a sensitively amplified microphone, which is fitted into the house as part of the service. This can be used even if the caller is unable to reach the telephone. The staff at the centre will then take action. Sometimes people are frightened and lonely in the middle of the night and just need reassurance. However, in the case of illness or accident the staff can take immediate action, using the personal information which comes up on the screen. This consists of a short medical history of the patient, the name and phone number of his or her general practitioner, information about the local support system and nearest key holder, and the names and phone numbers of sons or daughters, the local gardai, and ambulance and fire brigade. Experience in other countries indicates that in many cases no action is required other than to reassure the caller that they have a communication's link available to them at all times.

In Ireland this service operates all over the twenty-six counties, with a monitoring office centre in Dublin. The service is run by Contactors Homelink.

Contactors Homelink
Terry Byrne, General Manager
330 North Circular Road
Dublin 7
☎ Dublin 300244/300944

In Northern Ireland you will find a sister company, Helplink, at the following address.

Helplink
16 Wellington Park
Belfast BT9 6DJ
☎ 0232 681536

There are other alternatives for people who may feel they could do with something more simple and less expensive. You might, for example, like to consider a **mobile panic button**. These buttons are normally installed beside the bed in the main bedroom or beside the front door when your house alarm system is being put in. You can now, however, get a portable one, which you can carry around the house. If you need help suddenly, press the button; this will trigger off a signal through the telephone circuit that you need assistance. The button will not give you voice communication and it will not enable you to tell anyone the reason you need assistance, but it will tell people that you need help.

Or you might like to consider a solution suggested to me once by an elderly Co. Dublin man. He wrote that he was in his eighty-seventh year and living alone since his wife had died. He was, he said, 'slightly incapacitated with arthritis, high blood pressure and angina, but able to get my own breakfast and tea and with the aid of a stick manage a short walk of thirty minutes every day, weather permitting. I am also very fortunate to have an excellent home help who lives about one mile from me and who comes Monday through Friday to cook my dinner, clean the house and organise my shopping. I decided to purchase a **cordless telephone**. My main phone is in the hall and the base for the cordless phone is beside the bed. I carry the phone if I'm out in the garage or garden, or across the road to visit a neighbour – it has a range of 245 yards. When I retire at night I put it back on the base, as it is fitted with a rechargeable battery. Before doing this I dial my home help's number – she doesn't answer it – but if I need assistance all I have to do is lift the handset and press a button marked *Redial*.'

• electrical appliances – the golden rule

Bring electrical appliances back to the shop where you bought them. These outlets should be able to repair the appliance and do it free of charge if it is under guarantee, or in some cases replace it. If they are no longer in business, or no longer handling the appliance, they should be able to tell you where you can have it repaired. For those who don't know where an appliance was bought, or who cannot go back to the shop, service telephone numbers and addresses for repairs have been given under the brand name of specific appliances. In most cases these are the numbers and addresses of the head office, who will be able to organise the repair or give you the name of a local man who will assist you.

• electrical wiring

It is very important that you get a qualified person to do your electrical jobs. Bad and faulty wiring can cost lives. There are two associations of electrical contractors, the **Electrical Contractors' Association** and the **Association of Electrical Contractors of Ireland**. Both associations will be happy to give you a list of contractors who are members of their particular association. You can write to them or telephone them at the addresses given.

Electrical Contractors' Association
c/o Construction Industry Federation
Federation House
Canal Road
Dublin 6
☎ Dublin 977487

Association of Electrical Contractors of Ireland
McKinley House
Main Street
Blackrock
Co. Dublin
☎ Dublin 2886499

Register of contractors:

For some time now the Electrical Contractors' Association, the Association of Electrical Contractors of Ireland, the ESB, the Electro Technical Council of Ireland, and the Department of Energy have been working together to set up a Register of Electrical Contractors of Ireland – to be known as RECO. At the time of going to press, this was not yet in operation, but the register is expected to be available to the public by the middle of 1992. The office will be based at Parnell Avenue, Harold's Cross, Dublin 12.

For the names of contractors in Northern Ireland, you should contact the **National Inspection Council for Electrical Installation Contracting**, Vintage House, 37 Albert Embankment, London SE1 7UJ, ☎ 071 5827746.

• electrolux

Service:

Electroservice
Long Mile Road
Dublin 12
☎ Dublin 518666

Parts:

Charlie Shiels
Golden Bridge Industrial Estate
Inchicore
Dublin 8
☎ Dublin 545844

In Northern Ireland contact the following address.

Electrolux Tricity Bendix Service
Unit 3, Edenderry Industrial Estate
326 Crumlin Road
Belfast BT14 7EE
☎ 0232 746591

electropollution – you and your house

Have you ever thought that the house you are living in might be bad for you? There are people in this country and in many other countries who believe houses are often incompatible with the people who live in them. One man who has been researching this area for a number of years is Michael Quinn of Bohernabreena, Co. Dublin. 'The electric magnetic fields in the spot where a house is built can affect a person's health, so can the way a house is built and furnished. There's such a thing as a "healthy" house – and one that is unhealthy.

'Some houses suffer because they are built over granite, and others suffer from bad energy because of water underneath the house. These are called geopathic stresses; they are "bad energies", and they can affect the body in a variety of ways. In some households the husband is out all day working, the wife and young children are at home – and they have problems; he doesn't. It may affect their nervous system, it can make them tired and irritable and cause a variety of symptoms. Building biology is about building an organic house, with as much that is compatible with the human body as is possible.'

Michael is very concerned about the whole subject of electropollution – electromagnetic energy and its damaging effects. 'Electromagnetic energy is the energy given off by electric currents. It is produced by electric power lines, microwaves, fluorescent lighting, VDUs, telecommunications and even electric blankets. Electropollution is the damage caused to living creatures by electromagnetic energy.' From his home in Bohernabreena, Michael Quinn sells products which he says help to combat some of the effects of electropollution.

'In Germany they now have what is called a contact breaker, which they fit beside the fuse-box, and when you switch off the last light or piece of equipment at night, everything goes dead. No electricity goes through the wiring – except for the fridge and freezer which have to be bypassed. The rest of the wiring is neutralised, as it were, until you put on the first light the next morning. We can supply these contact breakers, and they do work.'

If you don't want to invest in a contact breaker, the very least you can do is pull out the plug of anything in the bedroom at night – the radio, the electric blanket. 'Bedrooms can give rise to problems because you are sleeping in them for such a long period. Electric blankets can be used to heat the bed, but then you should pull out the plug rather than turn them off.'

There are other products available, including an area neutraliser, 'which neutralises a house where there are problems – either electromagnetic stress or geopathic stress. And we have a pendant which is specifically designed to deal with bad energies – you wear it wherever you find the energies are unhealthy. People have had remarkable improvements in their energy levels as a result.'

You can contact **Michael Quinn** at Sunnyhill, Bohernabreena, Dublin 24, ☎ Dublin 513619.

• embossing on leather

If you want to emboss a leather briefcase, a wallet or perhaps a prayer book, **Des Breen** of **Antiquarian Bookcrafts Ltd**, Marlay Craft Courtyard, Marlay Park, Rathfarnham, Dublin 16, will do this for you. The cost works out at about £1 a letter. (There is a car-park right beside the courtyard – it's the first entrance as you come from Rathfarnham, immediately after the hockey grounds; the main public car-park is further on.) You can ring Des at ☎ Dublin 942834.

• emide domestic appliances

Noel McCabe Distributors
Bluebell Industrial Estate
Dublin 12
☎ Dublin 502926

In Northern Ireland these appliances are also serviced by Noel McCabe Distributors, direct from Dublin.

engraving

Kingscraft
Grafton Street
Cork
☎ 021 270034

Pat Buckley and **Don O'Mahony** are in Grafton Street in Cork – there *is* a Grafton Street in Cork, though most of the Cork people whom I asked didn't know about it and a few seemed almost indignant at the suggestion. It's just off Oliver Plunkett Street, at the Grand Parade End, really more of a lane than a street.

Many jewellers do machine engraving, but Pat and Don do their engraving freehand on silver and glass, in any particular script or lettering you happen to fancy. They use old steel tools called graves, which look like small chisels. They will also do designs, and they are experts on crests of all kinds. There is a vogue at the moment for signet rings with your own crest on them, but wherever you want your crest engraved – provided it's silver or glass – Don and Pat can do it for you.

Pat did his apprenticeship with Egan's, the famous old Cork firm; Don trained with Pat. Together they work under the name Kingscraft.

• entertaining (see parties and party accessories)

• expelair appliances

GEC Distributors
15 Hendrick Street
Dublin 7
☎ Dublin 775413
(*Republic of Ireland*)

Expelair
7-10 Prince Regent Road
Castlereagh
Belfast BT5 6QR
☎ 0232 401337
(*Northern Ireland*)
(will direct you to your nearest service agent)

• fagor appliances

Bluebell Appliance Service Ltd
Naas Road
Dublin 12
☎ Dublin 783955/508455

• fakir/nilco vacuum cleaners and polishers

Noel McCabe Distributors
Bluebell Industrial Estate
Dublin 12
☎ Dublin 502926

Noel McCabe Distributors also look after customers with Fakir/Nilco appliances in Northern Ireland.

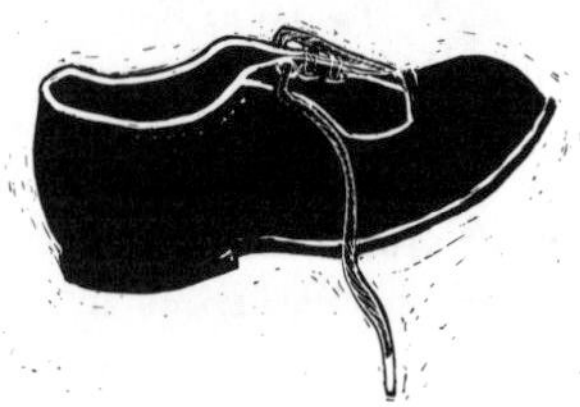

feet and footwear

Eddie Tutty makes shoes for problem feet, and many of the problem feet Eddie sees are female, and they belong to people who have worn the wrong kind of shoes for a long time. 'If you wear high heels over a long period of time, the metatarsal arch suffers badly, because it takes the brunt of the body weight. You can end up with bunions and knuckle toes. Most high-heeled shoes have pointed toes, and the toes get pushed into the shape of the point. Instead of the big toe being straight, it gets pushed over the other toes, and the foot gets out of shape, so that eventually people find it hard to get shoes that fit.'

Eddie says that there are some feet – very few feet – which can wear a high heel, 'but the majority of ladies are not suited to high heels. They shouldn't wear shoes that are more than an inch and three-quarters in height at the very most, and I prefer them to be just an inch or an inch and three-eighths in height.'

Tutty's have been making shoes by hand since 1943 when Eddie's father started the business. When you go to him, he makes a last of your foot. This last is a one-off expense – once the last has been made, it can be used with each new pair of shoes you order.

In general, men don't have problems with their feet from bad footwear. Men get their shoes made because they 'like the idea of a quality shoe' or because they have a particular problem due to arthritis or some congenital abnormality. Eddy says that the shoes worn by young people in recent years have been very sensible: 'flat shoes, laced shoes, shoes with room for the toes to move'. But suppose fashions change? 'Fashions could well change', said Eddie, and the next fashion forecast for female footwear is platform soles, 'which are terrible for the feet and even worse for the back. There are some which are well designed, but the vast majority don't allow the foot to bend, and this puts pressure on the spine and upsets the posture.'

Eddie is available for consultation at **Tutty's** in the Powerscourt Centre, Dublin, on Thursday from 12.30 p.m. to 5.00 p.m. – though the shop itself is open all week – and in Friary Road, Naas, Co. Kildare, every Tuesday and Wednesday from 2.00 p.m. until 5.00 p.m. You can also telephone for an appointment: Friary Road, Naas, ☎ 045 76879 and Powerscourt Centre, Dublin, ☎ Dublin 6796566.

Catherine McIntyre in the **Scholl Shoe Shop**, 59 Grafton Street, Dublin 2, ☎ Dublin 774117, also sees people with problem feet. 'Frequently, problems are due to people wearing the wrong size of shoe and the wrong shape of shoe. You have to be careful as well with hosiery and socks. If they are too tight you can end up with in-grown toe-nails.'

Quite a few of the problem feet belong to women in their fifties and 'go back to the stiletto age, when heels were very high and toes were very narrow. Some standard court shoes can still be very narrow. The good thing about the Doc Martins and the flat shoes which teenagers are wearing is that they allow their feet to develop.'

She thinks it a pity that many people who have their feet measured when they are growing up, never get them measured again once they start buying fashion shoes. They should, she says. Scholl's offer a free foot-examination service: they will take a print of your feet, watch you walking, measure your feet and diagnose any problems you may have. But not during lunch-hours, please; drop by before 12.00 p.m. or after 3.00 p.m. They also offer a full chiropody service, although you need to make an appointment – ☎ Dublin 774117.

Some children have special problems when it comes to footwear. **Cripps**, 4 Terenure Place, Dublin 6, ☎ Dublin 907237, can supply shoes for all age groups, from toddlers to adults. They provide an advisory and specialist fitting service for children with orthopaedic problems, and also stock wide-fitting shoes right up to the Start-Rite H fitting.

Shoe fitting in the home:

For any person in the Dublin area who is not mobile and who cannot travel to a shoe shop, **Cripps** will do fittings in houses or nursing homes. Telephone Cripps at ☎ Dublin 907237.

• ferguson appliances

Electroservice
Long Mile Road
Dublin 12
☎ Dublin 518666

fireplaces

The most popular fireplace now is the kind of fireplace they were throwing out twenty-five and thirty years ago – an old marble fireplace or a cast-iron Victorian fireplace with a tiled surround. Young people in particular, who buy Victorian- and Edwardian-style houses, are restoring old fireplaces instead of putting in new ones. Most old fireplaces *can* be cleaned. It just takes time and hard work. If you haven't got a Victorian fireplace but would like to own one, you can always buy a modern reproduction, search out an old one and restore it yourself, or buy an old one which has been restored by somebody else.

Christopher O'Neill & Sons Ltd, The Marble Works, Ballyogan Road, Carrickmines, Dublin 18, ☎ Dublin 2955910, sell genuine old fireplaces as well as new reproduction ones. They've been working with fireplaces for a long time – the third generation of O'Neills is now in the business. It was one of the O'Neills who gave me a recipe, many years ago, for **removing stains** from white marble fireplaces. The problem with marble is that it is porous, so any staining goes right into it and can be quite difficult to remove. First, wash down the fireplace with warm, soapy water to remove any surface dust. Then apply a paste to the fireplace with a tissue. Leave it on for two days. Take it off and apply fresh paste. You can repeat this three or four times, over a week or more, until you see the stains beginning to fade. However, if the fireplace is badly scorched or marked, it can be very difficult to remove the stain because the mark will have gone right through to the other side. This is one reason why fireplace manufacturers often put coloured marble on the actual hearth so that scorch marks won't be so obvious. If you have a fireplace which needs attention or restoration, the O'Neills will be happy to help.

A. J. Bell, 122 Botanic Road, Glasnevin, Dublin 9, ☎ Dublin 301777, sell a special kit for cleaning old fireplaces, and the Byrne family – who have run the business since 1939 – will tell you exactly how to go about it, depending on whether it is an old marble or an old cast-iron fireplace.

If it is a marble fireplace, you have to remove the grease and dirt accumulated over the years and clean it right down with a special kind of poultice material. If it is damaged, you can repair it with Isopan, which will look like the veins of black in white marble, and rub it down with fine emery paper. When you've removed all the muck and repaired it, put on a special wax, leave it for twenty-four hours and polish it off with the finest of steel wool. Just one word of warning: be sure it *is* a marble fireplace. Many Victorian fireplaces have a surround of marbled slate which looks and even feels like marble, with veins of white or red or grey. This is where disaster can strike. Several people have rung the Byrnes in tears, when what they thought was their marble mantelpiece disintegrated into grey slate after enthusiastic cleaning. Marbling was a particular Victorian skill that is becoming fashionable again.

Restoring a cast-iron fireplace can also be very rewarding. Most of the old ones have layers and layers of black paint on them – so many layers, in fact, that the original detail and casting on the fireplace may be completely obliterated. It can be quite exciting to discover that underneath all the paint, there is a pretty pattern to be revealed. Cleaning it down is a dirty job, however, and can take a lot of paint stripper and energetic work with a wire brush. Again, be careful. Many Victorian fireplaces have a surround of marbled slate. If you have an old fireplace which needs to be restored and you don't feel like doing the job yourself, then Bells will be happy to restore it for you.

Brian McElvaney in **Sugan Antiques**, 97 Francis Street, Dublin 8, ☎ Dublin 531948, restores and sells Victorian cast-iron fireplaces and keeps a very good range in stock. If you have one you want restored, Brian will do the job for you.

Cliffords of Gardiner Lane, Dublin 1, ☎ Dublin 746457, have been in the fireplace business since 1947. They make high-quality fireplaces in marble, tile and stone, and supply the private and public sector. They make to suit individual requirements and build for gas as well as solid fuel. They also stock parts for solid-fuel ranges.

James Harding Fireplaces in The Green, Gowran, Co. Kilkenny, ☎ 056 26177, do a wide range of fireplaces, but they are specialists in the many uses of marble and stone. They make new reproduction fireplaces and also clean and restore old fireplaces. They construct architectural turnings, such as balustrades and door columns – they restored all the balustrades for the top of the Custom House in Dublin – and make old-style marble hand basins, kitchen worktops and bar counters. They will tackle anything you want in stone, granite or marble.

• flavel leisure cookers

Electric cookers:

Ideal Service
Kylemore Park West
Ballyfermot
Dublin 10
☎ Dublin 6266720

Gas cookers:

For cookers run on Calor Kosangas there is a big network of service agents around the country. Any dealer stockist will have a list, and if you can't find one contact the following.

Calor Kosangas
Long Mile Road
Dublin 12
☎ Dublin 505000

If your cooker is run on Flogas Ergas contact Flogas Ltd.

Flogas Ltd
Dublin Road
Drogheda
Co. Louth
☎ 041 31041

If it is run on natural gas, contact your local gas company.

In Northern Ireland contact the following agents.

Calor Gas (Northern Ireland) Ltd
Airport Road West
Sydenham
Belfast BT3 9EE
☎ 0232 458466
(cookers run on Calor Kosangas)

Flogas (Northern Ireland) Ltd
Airport Road West
Belfast BT3 9ED
☎ 0232 732611
(cookers run on Flogas Ergas)

floors, sanding and sealing

This is a tedious and dirty job, involving quite a lot of energy and effort, even with an electric sander. If you don't do it properly the results will be disappointing.

Before you begin sanding at all, you have to make sure the floor is in a fit state and that all the nails in the floor are punched down. Otherwise, you will rip the sanding sheet every time you hit a nail. Use a pin punch and hammer, and remember that when you sand the floor you will be reducing the level slightly and that the nails will be more inclined to protrude. So hammer them down well.

If the boards have shrunk, and floorboards often do shrink with central heating, you can fill in the gaps. Filling in the gaps means less draughts and a more even appearance. Brummer, available in good DIY shops and home-decorating shops, is a very useful filler and lasts very well, but doing the filling is a penitential exercise. You have to fill each gap once, let it sink and then top it up. It takes many boring hours on your knees. Even on a relatively small floor it seems to take forever.

It is now quite easy to hire out a sander. Just remember that ideally you need two sanders: a big one and a little hand sander, the big one for the main areas of the floor, the small one for the edges and corners where the other won't reach. Alternatively, you could do these areas by hand. Be sure you know how to use the machines before you take them home. A good hire company will make certain that you understand everything necessary before you leave their premises. They will also supply you with the different grades of sandpaper – rough to take off the heavy surface dirt, medium to follow, and fine paper to finish off. Don't leave the hire shop without knowing exactly how to secure the sandpaper to the machine, because when the paper is not on properly it breaks and flies all over the place. And each sheet costs you money. You could end up throwing your hat at it, but you are still going to have to pay the hire on the machine. So get as much information as you can when you collect it.

When you are using your machine, remember to empty the dust bag regularly. Every time you stop the machine to change the paper you should also empty the dust bag. When it comes to sealing the floor, you can choose between a varnish or a two-pack plastic coating, such as Rustins make. Rustins is very tough and it dries very fast – you can apply additional coats in a matter of hours – but the fumes are strong, so you need to be very careful about ventilation while you're using it.

Before you seal it, the floor should be completely free from dust, which means brushing it first with a soft brush, then vacuuming it over and over again, and finally rubbing it over with white spirit. Any particles of dust or dirt which remain will be locked on to the floor when you put on the seal. The first coat of seal is best put on with a cloth, and the subsequent coats with a brush, and you should use a new brush which has never been used for anything else. You need a minimum of three coats, I think, and four is even better. But don't make the coats too thick.

In between each coat you should sand the floor very gently; just brush it slightly with fine sandpaper to provide a key for the next coat. It does make a difference. And, of course, after you sand it, vacuum up any dust.

If all this makes you feel less than enthusiastic about tackling the job, you might like to get it done professionally. Martin Kane has been working with floors since he was a teenager. The cost will depend on the area involved. Yes, it would be cheaper to do the job yourself – but can you face it? If you can't, contact **Martin Kane** at 88 Ballinteer Park, Dublin 16, ☎ Dublin 2984051.

Floors laid:

Hardwood Flooring Sales
Ian Guilfoyle
Collinstown Cross
Cloghran
Co. Dublin
☎ Dublin 8427366

• flymo appliances

Smurfit Packaging Systems
Ballymount Road
Walkinstown
Dublin 12
☎ Dublin 507266
(Republic of Ireland)

Flymo electric only:

Electrolux Tricity Bendix Service
Unit 3, Edenderry Industrial Estate
326 Crumlin Road
Belfast BT14 7EE
☎ 0232 746591
(Northern Ireland)

food

Like most mothers, it seems to me that a great deal of my life has been concerned with food – buying it, cooking it and clearing up after it. On average, there have always been nine or ten people to feed in our house, which is a lot of people and a lot of food, and it absorbs a very large proportion of our income.

It is my belief that some people, and virtually all young people, will eat anything in the fridge, in a press or in the larder. It doesn't necessarily mean they are hungry. I have frequently seen one teenage member of the family eat his way through a large three-course meal and sit down less than an hour later to several bowls of cereal. I have seen another demolish an entire loaf of bread in the course of an evening and still complain of feeling peckish before bedtime.

There are certain foods which are apparently irresistible. Cereals are always sure to vanish fast, but yoghurt, cooked ham, cheese of any kind, bread and rolls, fruit juice, cartons of Petit Filous, cream, and nuts all have a short life. I have found that unless I hide them they simply vanish. I hide yoghurt so that it will still be there as a dessert after dinner, and not all eaten in mid-afternoon. I hide ham and cheese so that I will have them the following morning. I have so often bought six or eight slices of ham, precisely what I might need to make lunches or a pack of easy singles for toasted cheese at breakfast time, only to discover that when I went to make the lunches or the breakfast I had only a slice-and-a-half of ham and two of cheese left. Who took them? Who, indeed. Not I, not I, not I.

I buy walnuts to put in brown soda bread, but very often there are none left when I go to look for them. I have one son who can eat walnuts by the packet.

When I complained on one particular occasion he said rather querulously, 'You have them hidden all over the house, and now I'm afraid to eat them because I don't know how long you've left them there, and they're not nice and crunchy any more.'

I hide bread and rolls: the rolls for lunches, the bread for breakfast. But still they vanish, and every so often I blow my top. I realised recently that people who didn't know me might think me distinctly odd; I had six Petit Filous hidden behind the filing cabinet in my study (they're nice for packed lunches), I had hidden cheese in the broom cupboard, nuts in my wardrobe, the rolls in a high press and the biscuits for lunches in along with the paint.

On one memorable occasion quite a number of years ago I got really rattled about the disappearance of some bread rolls. At the time we were making seven packed lunches a day, and I had bought the rolls as a special treat. Having spent most of the day in the garden I came into the house in the late afternoon. I went to make lunches for the next day and found that every bit of bread in the bread bin was gone, and more than half the rolls. Nobody, of course, had taken them. On similar occasions in the past I had almost been persuaded that I was imagining things. This time I was determined that I was not going to end up wondering if I'd really only bought four rolls instead of nine. I vowed I'd find out where the five missing rolls had gone. No food, I said, certainly no bread of any kind, until I found out who took the rolls.

Hunger didn't set in for a while, but by late evening inquiries were being made about food. There was nothing to eat, I was told. I renewed my questions about the missing rolls. My second daughter admitted to taking one. My second son said he was sure she had taken two, and an acrimonious argument ensued, during which she said he never told the truth anyway, and he said he was sure he'd seen her taking two, and she finally produced a paperback Bible and swore she'd only taken one. I said I didn't think the Bible should be used in such arguments.

At this point my eldest son offered to make biscuits, and I said no, there was no margarine anyway, and he definitely couldn't use butter, nor could he make griddle cakes or buns. Nor had we any puff pastry to make sausage rolls, and I certainly wasn't going to go out and buy some bread. I said all I wanted was the truth; I would be happy just to know the truth.

'Well, then', said my eldest son. 'I took two.'

'And so did I', said my second daughter.

'And so did I', said the third.

'You're all liars,' said I, 'because that adds up to six, and there are only five missing. And *you* swore on the Bible that you'd only taken one.'

'I had my fingers crossed', said she, 'and my feet.'

'This is all ludicrous', said my eldest son. 'We tell the woman where they went and she won't believe us.'

'Actually I did tell the truth the first time', said my second daughter. 'I wouldn't tell a lie on the Bible.'

At which point my second son produced his youngest brother, then aged five. 'He says he took one', he said, holding him by the scruff of the neck.

'Unlikely,' said I, 'since they were in a high press.'

'I was only messing', said the five-year-old. 'I didn't take any.'

They then decided that the culprit was probably their eldest sister, who brought a packed lunch with her when she went out to meet a friend. 'I did not', she said when she returned home. 'I didn't even know they were there.'

Later I heard them discussing things in the room next to the kitchen. Somebody got the bright idea that father was the culprit. 'You know how absent-minded he is sometimes. He probably ate them and didn't know he was eating them.' This suggestion brought an explosive response from father.

Ten years later, I still don't know who took those rolls. Food continues to disappear, and most mothers will understand why I get mad when somebody says, 'There's never any food in this house.'

Food shop:

The Ballymaloe Shop in Ballymaloe, Co. Cork, ☎ 021 652032, is run by yet another Allen – Wendy. In this shop you will find all kinds of unusual food stuffs, including Balsamic vinegar, Italian olive oils from small producers, unrefined walnut and hazelnut oils, pink peppercorns, natural almond and vanilla essences, and natural food colourings, as well as jams, jellies and preserves.

• franke taps, sinks and hobs

F. E. Smith Electrical Ltd
3/5 Camden Place
Dublin 2
☎ Dublin 751702
(*Republic of Ireland*)

Euro Serv (Ireland) Ltd
66 Dows Road
Drumbo
Belfast BT8 8LB
☎ 0232 826446

Bodell Distributors Ltd
Hull's Lane
Moira Road
Lisburn
Co. Antrim BT28 2SR
☎ 0846 672412
(*Northern Ireland*)

• freezer bags and wrappings

K. & M. Evans
28 Mary's Abbey
Dublin 7
☎ Dublin 726855

• frigidaire refrigerators

K. T. Distributors
Unit 2, Baloo Crescent
Balloo Industrial Estate
Bangor
Co. Down BT19 2YX
☎ 0247 270130

• frister and rossman sewing machines

Sew-Knit Machine Centre
26 Bridge Street
Lisburn BT28 1XY
☎ 0846 601200

furniture repairs

McKeons at 1 Dolphin Market, Dublin 8,☎ Dublin 541276/541829, will tackle all kinds of furniture problems, from recovering garden seats to restoring antique pieces. I know. I had a very heavy, old cast-iron swinging garden seat, with sprung cushions and wooden arms. McKeons found exactly the kind of sailcloth I wanted, refurbished everything most handsomely and gave me back a seat which will give me pleasure and delight to the end of my days. I have seen armchairs and sofas which they have re-upholstered impeccably, and I have seen antique pieces which they have restored with care. Much of their work is domestic, but they also have worked for Dublin City Hall, the Mansion House and for court buildings.

M. J. O'Toole & Sons, Ltd, Roger's Lane, Lower Baggot Street, Dublin 2, ☎ Dublin 762536/761763, are a long-established firm; there have been O'Tooles making furniture in Baggot Street since 1901. O'Toole's do reproduction pieces and also repair and restore; once again, the emphasis is on care and craftsmanship.

For Karl O'Reilly, family furniture and furniture restoration have always been a valued part of life. Karl's uncles worked for the prestigious Hicks firm, and one uncle now works with Karl in the repair and restoration business his father started many years ago. The O'Reillys specialise in restoring antique furniture. Making old pieces beautiful again is something in which they take enormous pride and pleasure. 'We really enjoy our work', Karl says. He also has a big collection of unusual antique fittings for furniture. You will find **Karl O'Reilly** at 24 Clarence Mangan Road, South Circular Road, Dublin 8, ☎ Dublin 536930.

R. Phelan & Sons in Ballybought Street, Kilkenny (off the Comer Road, opposite the military barracks in Kilkenny town), ☎ 056 62338, are specialists in restoring antique furniture. This business was started by Richard Phelan over sixty years ago. There are six Phelans in the business today: three of Richard's sons, Dony, Paddy and Eugene, and two of his grandsons, Aidan and Richard. There is also a brother-in-law, Christy Delany. The Phelans are devoted to high-quality furniture restoration and do things the old way. They don't, for example, use foam rubber in their stuffing, they use horsehair – they bought up all the old hair mattresses they could find and say that they have enough to last for twelve years at least. After that, they're not sure what they will do. They use no spray or varnish;

everything is French polished. If a part is missing, they make one to match. The Phelans tackle big jobs and small.

You may also wish to contact the following.

Patrick Boyle (IPCRA)
Marlay Craft Courtyard
Marlay Park
Grange Road
Dublin 16
☎ Dublin 936989

Patrick Cabourne-Basset
(IPCRA)
The Farmhouse
Sarsfield's Court
Glanmire
Co. Cork
☎ 021 821076 (after 6.00 p.m.)

Karl and Claire Davenport
(IPCRA)
Kilbrook
Enfield
Co. Meath
☎ 0405 41214

• furniture repair parts

Unusual screws, hinges and fittings:

Modern Veneer Importers Ltd
26 Wolfe Tone Street
Dublin 1
☎ Dublin 732133/ 732906/ 732515

• futura appliances

Ideal Service
Kylemore Park West
Ballyfermot
Dublin 10
☎ Dublin 6266720

Rafferty & Tomany
3a The Mall
Newry
Co. Down BT34 1BX
☎ 0693 66550
(*Northern Ireland*)

• gaelwood-phoenix conversion units

These units are for converting solid-fuel cookers to oil.

Multiheat
179 James Street
Dublin 8
☎ Dublin 712976/714641
(*Republic of Ireland*)

• gaggenau appliances

F. E. Smith Electrical Ltd
3/5 Camden Place
Dublin 2
☎ Dublin 751702
(*Republic of Ireland*)

Kee (Hospital) Services
46 Bradbury Place
Belfast BT7 1RU
☎ 0232 322916
(*Northern Ireland*)

garden centres

Many gardeners read about particular plants, shrubs or trees which they would like, but find when they go to their local garden centre that the plants are often not available.

A Guide to Garden Centres and Nurseries in Ireland was produced by the Consumer's Association of Ireland in collaboration with the Irish Garden Plant Society. It not only gives the names and addresses of centres all over Ireland, North and South, but also gives details of the particular plants in which they specialise. Altogether, some 129 nurseries and garden centres are listed. The guide contains no advertising – the information is based on independent research – and for good measure it is printed on recycled paper.

You can obtain a copy from the **Consumer's Association of Ireland**, 45 Upper Mount Street, Dublin 2, for £3.20 including postage.

• garden pots

Michael Roche
Kiltrea Bridge Pottery
Kiltrea Bridge
Enniscorthy
Co. Wexford
☎ 054 35107

Paddy Murphy
Carley's Bridge
Enniscorthy
Co Wexford
☎ 054 35443

• gas appliances

Remember that gas appliances and gas heating systems can be dangerous if not properly installed and maintained by qualified personnel, and that gas appliances should only be serviced by accredited service agents.

• gas heaters

There is a big network of service agents around the country for gas heaters run on Calor Kosangas. Any dealer stockist will have a list. If you can't find one contact **Calor Kosangas**, Long Mile Road, Dublin 12, ☎ Dublin 505000.

If your heater is run on Flogas Ergas contact **Flogas Ltd**, Dublin Road, Drogheda, Co. Louth, ☎ 041 31041.

If your heater is run on natural gas, contact your local natural gas company.

In Northern Ireland contact **Calor Gas (Northern Ireland) Ltd**, Airport Road West, Sydenham, Belfast BT3 9EE, ☎ 0232 458466, if your heater is run on Calor Kosangas.

If it is run on Flogas Ergas, contact **Flogas (Northern Ireland) Ltd**, Airport Road West, Belfast BT3 9ED, ☎ 0232 732611.

• general electric, large appliances

Appliance Network Service
19 East Essex Street
Dublin 2
☎ Dublin 715528/6795244

• gilded furniture, frames and mirrors, restored

Cresten Doherty
45 Grange Court
Rathfarnham
Dublin 14
☎ Dublin 941639

Cathy Carrigan (IPCRA)
50 Park Avenue
Dublin 4
☎ Dublin 2692521

Anne Hyland (IPCRA)
Beechmount
Roscrea
Co. Tipperary
☎ 0505 22310

Susan Mulhall (IPCRA)
Blackwood
Roberstown
Co. Kildare
☎ 045 60336

Emily Naper (IPCRA)
Lough Crew
Oldcastle
Co. Meath
☎ 049 41356

Wlodek Szustkiewicz (IPCRA)
Stacumny House
Celbridge
Co. Kildare
☎ Dublin 6288345, ext. 10

• glen electric heating appliances

Dimpco Ltd
Airport Road
Cloghran
Dublin 9
☎ Dublin 8428222

In Northern Ireland, to find the name of your nearest service person, contact Brownbrook Distributors.

Brownbrook Distributors Ltd
Unit 24, Seagoe Industrial Estate
Portadown
Co. Armagh BT63 5TH
☎ 0762 337317

• goblin vacuum cleaners

Beaumark Service Company
2a Sunbury Industrial Estate
Walkinstown
Dublin 12
☎ Dublin 504620

In Northern Ireland **CareElectric** will look after you. CareElectric is a province-wide network of experienced service electricians, co-ordinated by a mobile telephone link to the headquarters of Northern Ireland Electricity. They are on call Monday to Friday and you can telephone them from anywhere in Northern Ireland at the local call rate. The number to ring for service on larger appliances is ☎ 0345 616744. In the case of a smaller appliance, such as a vacuum cleaner, you can bring it in to your local ShopElectric where they will forward it to the CareElectric Central Workshop.

• goldstar appliances

V. Leonard & Co Ltd
44a Alliance Avenue
Belfast BT14 7LX
☎ 0232 749326

• golf caddy cars

For Powakaddys and most other caddy cars:

F. E. Smith Electrical Ltd
3/5 Camden Place
Dublin 2
☎ Dublin 7517021

• gorenje appliances

Ideal Service
Kylemore Park West
Ballyfermot
Dublin 10
☎ Dublin 6266720

• grave care

Grave Care is a service which does exactly what you would expect – looks after graves for people who may not have the time, or may not live near enough, to do the job themselves. You will find them at 1 Church Road, Malahide, Co. Dublin, ☎ Dublin 8451534 /8453615.

• grundig equipment

Grundig Ireland Ltd
Unit 9, Western Industrial Estate
Naas Road
Dublin 12
☎ Dublin 509366
(*Republic of Ireland*)

Craigavon TV Service
17 Logan Drive
Lurgan
Craigavon
Co. Armagh BT66 8DA
☎ 0762 326119/322505
(*Northern Ireland*)

• guitars

Danvel
Marlay Craft Courtyard
Marlay Park
Grange Road
Rathfarnham
Dublin 16
☎ Dublin 942741

Derrick Nelson of Danvel makes all kinds of guitars – steel-string accoustic guitars, nylon-string classical guitars, jazz guitars, and electric guitars and basses. His guitars are purchased by some of the top names on the music scene; he also repairs.

hair problems

Saks
15 Sackville Place
Dublin 12
☎ Dublin 786344

Saks provide all the usual hairdressing services, but they also specialise in making wigs and hair pieces. If, because of medical treatment, you may temporarily lose your hair, Saks recommend that you go along and see them *before* treatment. This way, if you should need a hairpiece or a wig, they can be sure of matching it with your own hair.

Hair care has become a much more elaborate business than it was when I was growing up, and the potential for experimentation is enormous. We have had one particularly enthusiastic amateur hairdresser in the family who could never resist an opportunity to try out his skills. His most spectacular experiment took place one December, a few weeks before Christmas. He found a highlight kit which had been sent to me as a gift – it was for highlighting your hair in your own home. I had put it away and forgotten all about it until I came home one night to find various members of the family sitting in the kitchen, wreathed in gleeful smiles. The amateur hairdresser was missing. 'You should see his hair', said one of his sisters. 'When he stood behind me I could see his reflection in the microwave, and he actually *glowed*', said another. And they all fell around the place laughing.

He had, it appeared, got hold of my highlight kit and decided to do a job on his hair. He wanted to go really gold, and since his natural colour is black, he had felt the best way of doing a good job was to leave the solution on for twice the recommended length of time – or was it three times? The result, I was given to understand, had to be seen to be believed.

I didn't get a chance to see it that evening because he never appeared. The next morning I went up to his room, curious to know if the reports were factual, but there was a large notice on his door saying, 'No, you cannot see my hair.' I could still view some of his handiwork, however, when I learned that a younger brother, who had been in bed when I came home, had also got a dose of highlights. When I excavated him out from under the duvet, he didn't look too bad at all – just flicks of pale gold on the front of his dark hair. In fact, I decided I quite liked it.

When I finally got to see the perpetrator late the following evening, the vivid descriptions had not been exaggerated. Vivid was the operative word: vivid sunset orange, vivid canary yellow and streaks of ruddy chestnut. I could understand perfectly why he was sitting so sheepishly in a corner and had refused to put his nose, let alone his head, outside the door of the house. When he had stayed in for the best part of a week, and it looked like I was going to have him home forever, I gave in and sent him along to friends in Saks. They got him back almost to normal again; and if he had done an even more drastic job on his hair and killed it off altogether, they could have made him a very nice wig.

• handicapped / the disabled, services for

There are a number of people who specialise in aids of various kinds, from gadgets which make it easier to do basic household chores, to heavier equipment, such as lifts and hoists. If you have been in hospital, the occupational therapist will have given you advice and information on your needs. Outside a hospital, if you need help you can get in touch with your local health board to see if they have a community occupational therapist who can advise you. Or you can contact the National Rehabilitation Board.

National Rehabilitation Board
25 Clyde Road
Dublin 4
☎ Dublin 684181

The Rehabilitation Board has specially trained staff who are familiar with the wide range of aids and services available, and who can advise people on what would be best suited to individual requirements.

Among the firms which specialise in handicapped and disabled aids and equipments are the following.

The Arthritis Foundation of Ireland
1 Clanwilliam Square
Grand Canal Quay
Dublin 2
☎ Dublin 618188

Fannin Healthcare
14-16 Redmond's Hill
Dublin 2
☎ Dublin 782211

Fannin Healthcare
9 Washington Street
Cork
☎ 021 274011

Fannin Healthcare
31 Dominick Street
Galway
☎ 091 63882

Liberty Aids and Lifts
Grantham House
Lower Camden Street
Dublin 8
☎ Dublin 783922

Mobility Aids Ltd
Unit 2, 78 Walkinstown Road
Dublin 12
☎ Dublin 568536

PEI Surgical
13 Fade Street
Dublin 2
☎ Dublin 770142/774042

In Northern Ireland you can contact the **Northern Ireland Council on Disability**, 2 Annadale Avenue, Belfast BT7 3UR, ☎ 0232 491011. The council is a development agency interested in improving the quality of life of people with disabilities. It will refer people to the most appropriate source of information and also offers some specific services – the council runs a driving school for disabled people and supplies general information on transport and mobility.

If you want specific information on particular aids you should contact the **Regional Disablement Services**, Musgrave Park Hospital, Belfast, ☎ 0232 669501, ext. 2700. This is an umbrella organisation for a number of different centres – the Disabled Living Centre, the Wheelchair Centre, the Communication Advice Centre, the Artificial Limbs Centre and the Northern Ireland Orthopaedic Service. The organisation has a permanent display of all the aids and equipment available in Northern Ireland. It isn't a retail shop as such, but you can look at what's available, get expert advice on what would best suit your needs and information on where to buy it. A visit is by appointment only.

I think it's also worth mentioning **swimming aids. White Leather Industries Ltd** in Waterford are essentially a manufacturer of leather garments. Since May 1989, however, they have been making swimming aids for young children. The aids are intended for children from four months to seven years. They are made from nylon lycra and have built-in floats which are made of polystyrene. They come in two styles: a swimming band and a swimming suit.

David White, the managing director of White Leather Industries, says they have sold them into sports shops in towns all over Ireland, and have found, to their surprise, that they are particularly suitable for handicapped children. If you want to find out more about these aids, contact **David White** at the following address.

White Leather Industries
Unit 6, Enterprise Centre
High Street
Waterford
☎ 051 70688

• hands for hire

Hands for Hire Ltd
Multi-Service Agency
1 Church Road
Malahide
Co. Dublin
☎ Dublin 8451534/8453615

Roisin Naughton, who runs Hands for Hire, says she has people on her books who will tackle almost any job, from electrical work to nursing, ironing, translation, secretarial work, driving, child care, leaflet delivery, gardening, and tree cutting.

• harps

Colm O Meachair, in Marlay Craft Courtyard, Marlay Park, Grange Road, Rathfarnham, Dublin 16, ☎ Dublin 942806, specialises in making Irish harps. He also repairs and restores them.

• harpsichords, repaired and restored

Hugo Vegter (IPCRA)
Ivy Cottage
Glenmore
Cobh
Co. Cork
☎ 021 813352

• heating

Heating consultants:

Most of the heating consultancy firms in Ireland work chiefly on commercial and industrial projects. One man who concentrates on domestic heating is **Bob Couchman**, Cherry Lodge, Killincarrig, Delgany, Co. Wicklow, ☎ Dublin 2876774/2800744.

Among the people who handle domestic jobs as well as the bigger industrial and commercial projects are the following.

J. W. Hogan and Associates
62 Ranelagh Village
Dublin 6
☎ Dublin 978854

Delap & Waller
Bloomfield House
Bloomfield Avenue
Dublin 8
☎ Dublin 534031

In Northern Ireland, contact these firms.

McMichael Energy Services
13 Front Road
Drumbo
Lisburn BT27 5JZ
☎ 0232 826353
(note: this address may change by autumn 1992)

Brian Page
Institute of Domestic Heating and Environmental Engineers
17 Erinvale Avenue
Belfast BT10 OFN
☎ 0232 612867

All of these firms employ consulting engineers who are qualified to investigate heating problems and who can support your case in court if necessary. You can, however, get very good advice from men who may not be heating engineers but who have worked all their lives in the heating field and have gained wide experience. Two are listed below.

Jimmy Rushe
12 Lower Kennelsfort Road
Palmerstown
Dublin 20
☎ Dublin 6262229

Joe Manifold
40 Sundrive Road
Kimmage
Dublin 12
☎ Dublin 967355

Heating installers:

You can obtain lists of heating installers from the following.

Mechanical Engineering and Building Services Contractors Association
c/o Construction Industry Federation
Federation House
Canal Road
Dublin 6
☎ Dublin 977487

Irish Domestic Heating & Environmental Engineers Association
c/o Anne Mullin
103 The Crescent
Millbrook Lawns
Tallaght
Dublin 24
☎ Dublin 757132 (daytime)
☎ Dublin 526426 (evenings)

Designed Heating
c/o Bill Penrice
102 Trees Road
Mount Merrion
Co. Dublin
☎ Dublin 2884850/2884851

Options:

Ideally, if you have been planning to install a new heating system or want to change the one you already have, you should do it during the warm summer months. But as any heating engineer or installer will tell you, very few people go about things in an ideal way. The majority tend to think of heating when they see winter approaching and when the prospect of bleak days and cold nights seems only too real.

Domestic heating is about keeping pleasantly and comfortably warm. But how warm is that? Different people and different rooms in the house require different degrees of heat. As a rule, people over the age of sixty-five need a surrounding temperature of not less than 18°C to stay warm. Small babies probably need even more warmth than that, and toddlers who live on or near the floor are also a special case – a head-height temperature of 18°C for adults doesn't mean that the temperature is the same down there in the toddler's world.

The idea of heating all the rooms in the house is a relatively recent one in these islands, but even if you have heat available right through the house, the heat requirements will also vary from one room to another, depending on the main use to which the room is put. When bedrooms first came to be heated people were happy with a temperature of 10°C. But over the years the acceptable level has moved up, until today most people would like it to be 15°C, and in some countries even higher temperatures are preferred. The acceptable comfortable temperature in a living-room area is now 21°C. Bathrooms obviously need to be warm or capable of being warmed quickly. People may not necessarily spend a long time having a bath, but they need a warm room while they're there – between 21°C and 23°C. A wall-mounted fan heater is ideal for producing this kind of quick heat.

What are the heating options?

Basically, you can choose between oil, natural gas, LPG (liquid petroleum gas), electricity or solid fuel. There are a number of reasons why **oil** is attractive as a heating system. It is, for example, a very clean and efficient way of heating your house. It is an ideal system for people who are out during the day and want instant heat when they come home in the evening, or for an hour or two after they get up in the morning. Oil is very easily maintained; the very minimum of service attention is all it usually requires. It is easily stored in a tank which takes up relatively little space. And it goes without saying that oil is a clean fuel environmentally and avoids the environmental damage associated with other fuels.

As a native fuel under the control of the state, **natural gas** is a great national asset. Its availability is not dependent on the political situation elsewhere, and by using natural gas instead of imported fuels we are improving the national balance of payments. Natural gas, furthermore, is clean, reliable and very efficient. It is a fuel which requires no preparation of any kind for combustion. Appliances can be simple and still very reliable. A small boiler, which can fit unobtrusively under a kitchen worktop or slot on to the kitchen wall between presses, can produce between 40,000 to 60,000 BTUs of heat and hot water – enough for an average semi-detached house. And it works very quietly, so that it doesn't intrude in any way in the kitchen scene. It is clear that natural gas is a splendidly clean fuel which can play a major role in reducing air pollution and in improving the urban environment.

People in rural areas may not have access to natural gas, but for many years cooking by **liquid petroleum gas (LPG)** has been a country tradition, particularly in country areas where electricity cuts were likely to occur from time to time. Almost 30 per cent of Irish homes use bottled gas as their primary method of cooking. LPG is the term used to describe a number of different gases which are the normal constituents of crude-oil refining. Frequently, it is also found in association with natural gas. LPG is available either from oil-producing countries or refineries and is totally non-polluting in both its liquid and gaseous forms; on combustion it has the same clean burning aspects as natural gas.

The idea of an LPG heating system has only become more widespread in recent years. It can operate as a complete home-energy system, supplying not only heat but hot water and controllable cooking. All you need is a storage tank, which can be placed in a convenient spot in your garden, or a 'bank' of large cylinders stored outdoors and piped to the relevant appliance or appliances.

Maintenance on an LPG system is minimal. Systems can be designed to suit individual needs, and if you want to link it in with an existing solid-fuel system, this can also be done though it will cost you a bit more. It must be said, however, that LPG can be an expensive fuel to use for heating your home.

Electricity is a clean and convenient source of energy. It is pollution free, kind to the environment and there is no fuel to order, no boiler house, no fuel store and no flues to worry about. Every house has a supply on tap. Electricity is not the cheapest source of energy, but electricity companies will argue that if you choose your appliances with care and avail of the economy rate night meter, then heating will work out economically.

Night storage heating uses electricity at less than half the standard price to provide a steady heat during the daylight hours, typically in living-rooms and in halls. Modern storage heaters are slim and elegant and blend in happily with a modern or traditional decor. They are easily installed, since they need no plumbing – just simple wiring circuits back to the meter position. Once installed, they are virtually maintenance free and will build up a sure supply of heat for your home while the household is asleep.

When oil prices went up many people installed a **solid-fuel** heating system. Quite a few continue to live with the system happily, but others undoubtedly found that they got more than they bargained for. A solid-fuel system doesn't necessarily suit everybody, and anybody who is considering installing one should consider what it will involve before they make a decision.

Involve is perhaps the operative word. An oil-fired, electrical or gas system doesn't really involve the user very much at all: it works with the minimum of attention. A solid-fuel system will demand much more of you and your time and depend upon the space at your disposal. You will need, for example, a place in which to store it, and solid fuel in any form or quantity takes up quite a bit of room. You will also have to fuel it on a regular basis. How regularly depends on the fuel you use, but even the fuels with the most efficient output, like the higher grades of anthracite, will require replenishing at least several times in every twenty-four hours. Every solid-fuel appliance needs to be kept clean. It needs the ashpan emptied before it gets too full, or the fire won't work properly, and this can mean emptying it several times a day if you have a solid-fuel cooker, depending on the fuel. In addition, the internal flueways of any solid-fuel appliance need to be thoroughly cleaned at regular intervals, or again you won't get good heat, and this is dirty work.

I mention this because these are all aspects of a solid-fuel system which should be considered before installing one. However, a solid-fuel system has advantages as well as disadvantages. Most heating systems which use oil, gas or electricity are programmed to come on only for certain periods of the day. A solid-fuel system enables you to have heat right around the clock; it means you can have a warm house at any time of the day – and this can be important if there are people in the house all the time, like babies and young children, or elderly people who feel the cold.

Solid-fuel heating can be in the form of a back boiler, a cooker, a closed appliance of some form or other, or a stove. With any heating system it is important to have good controls. The right controls mean that you use your heat and energy as efficiently and effectively as possible, which in turn implies that you don't use more than you need to get the results you want. Good heating controls can save you a great deal of money.

Whichever system you decide upon, it is essential that it be properly installed. Any appliance is only as good as its installation. Getting good advice by consulting a good heating consultant or contractor can make all the difference between choosing the right system or choosing a bad one in the first place.

Heating systems cleaned:

Domestic Cleaning Services clean chimneys.

Kevin Ward
Domestic Cleaning Services
153 Glenmaroon Road
Dublin 20
☎ Dublin 6268217

• hiring equipment (see sam hire)

• hitachi

AV Imports
John F. Kennedy Drive
Bluebell
Dublin 12
☎ Dublin 504855

To get the name of your nearest service dealer in Northern Ireland for Hitachi tvs, videos and audio equipment, contact **V. Leonard & Co. Ltd**, 44a Alliance Avenue, Belfast BT14 7LX, ☎ 0232 749326.

For Hitachi domestic appliances in Northern Ireland, contact **Homecare Appliance Service,** Abbey Trading Estate, Longwood Road, Newtownabbey, Belfast BT36 7LD, ☎ 0232 365487.

• hoover

Service:

Hoover Ltd
Unit 119
Dublin Industrial Estate
Ballyboggan Road
Glasnevin, Co. Dublin
☎ Dublin 301666

Parts:

Charlie Shiels
Golden Bridge Industrial Estate
Inchicore
Dublin 8
☎ Dublin 545844

Service dealers all over Northern Ireland are listed on a full-page advertisement in the Northern Ireland BT telephone directory.

• hotpoint appliances

Hotpoint Service
Unit 49, Airways Industrial Estate
Dublin 17
☎ Dublin 8426088

In Northern Ireland, Hotpoint washing machines, tumble dryers and refrigerators are available from the following address.

Hotpoint Service
256 Ormeau Road
Belfast BT7 2FZ
☎ 0232 647111

Hotpoint microwaves and gas hobs are available in Northern Ireland from CredaCare.

CredaCare
256 Ormeau Road
Belfast BT7 2FZ
☎ 0232 641401

house buying

Buying a house is a big event in anybody's life, and for most people it is one of the biggest purchases they will ever make. Many people prefer to buy an old house rather than a new one, but when you buy an old house you can also be buying problems. Obviously, if you are buying through a building society or a bank, they will send out their own surveyor to check on the house and assure themselves that it is worth the amount of the mortgage. But this will not be an in-depth survey. Building societies always recommend that a purchaser have a detailed structural survey carried out by a competent person. You may, for instance, have your heart set on the house of your dreams, but a dream can turn into a nightmare if you find, after you move in, that there are major problems, such as beetle infestation, dry rot, wet rot, cracking of walls, leaking roofs, rising dampness or condensation.

Joseph Curtis is a chartered building surveyor and a professional associate of the **Royal Institution of Chartered Surveyors**. He works completely independently and is not tied to any building society or business firm. He feels very strongly that the cost of a detailed structural survey of a house can be a small price to pay for the assurance that the house you hope to buy has no faults or problems which are likely to cost you money in the future. A good chartered surveyor will examine everything that is reasonably visible: roof spaces where there are trap-doors, and outside roofs with ladders where this is possible. He will lift trap-doors in floors and, with the owner's consent, take up sample floorboards to inspect under the floors.

His inspection will cover the structure and finishes of the building, outbuildings, garden fences, walls and nearby trees which might cause damage to the building. It will also include a survey of the water services and drainage, and probably the central heating and hot-water systems. He provides a detailed report on his findings.

You can write to **Joseph Curtis** at 23 Upper Mount Street, Dublin 2, or telephone him at ☎ Dublin 766516.

Colm O'Reilly is an engineer who has worked in the building industry all his life. His company, **Beech Homes Ltd**, built over 130 houses in Dublin and Co. Kildare in small lots, and he has also done a lot of contract work over the years. He was a council member of the Irish Home Builders' Association for fifteen years and a founder director of the National House Building Guarantee Scheme.

Colm has set up what he calls a report service for people who are thinking of buying a house, whether it is a newly built house or an older one. The service is in the form of a snag list for new houses and an assessment of the structure and quality of older houses. If you are buying a second-hand home, Colm gives it a thorough inspection, 'from the sewerage and the foundations to the water penetration, the roofs and the structure – the whole house – I go over it very carefully and then give my report. I also help to assess the price when repair costs have to be taken into account.'

When Colm draws up a snag list on a new house, the purchaser can give the list to the builder so that he is obliged to hand over a properly completed house before the sale closes, and 'I find if the builder receives a sensible list from the engineer he appreciates the service.' You can contact **Colm O'Reilly** at 10 Vesey Park, Lucan, Co. Dublin, ☎ Dublin 6280156.

• husqvarna

Boiler parts:

Multiheat
179 James Street
Dublin 8
☎ Dublin 712976
(Republic of Ireland)

Rafferty & Tomany
3a The Mall
Newry
Co. Down BT34 1BX
☎ 0693 66550
(Northern Ireland)

Sewing machines:

Sew-Knit Machine Centre
26 Bridge Street
Lisburn BT28 1XY
☎ 0846 601200

Microwave cookers:

Electroservice
Long Mile Road
Dublin 12
☎ Dublin 518666

Dishwashers, cookers and hobs:

Electrolux Tricity Bendix Service
Unit 3, Edenderry Industrial Estate
326 Crumlin Road
Belfast BT14 7EE
☎ 0232 746591

• hygena ovens, hobs and refrigerators

Ideal Service
Kylemore Park West
Ballyfermot
Dublin 10
☎ Dublin 6266720
(services Republic of Ireland and Northern Ireland)

- ## ideal kettles, cooker hoods and hobs

Charlie Shiels
Golden Bridge Industrial Estate
Inchicore
Dublin 8
☎ Dublin 545844

- ## indesit appliances

Bluebell Appliance Service Ltd
Naas Road
Dublin 12
☎ Dublin 783955/508455
(*Republic of Ireland*)

Merloni Domestic Appliances Ltd
35 Little Donegal Street
Belfast BT1 2JD
☎ 0232 242420
(*Northern Ireland*)

insulation

You can install the best heating system available, but you are not going to get any value from it if all your heat escapes out into the cold air. One of the greatest energy wasters in some houses, however, has nothing to do with the roof, the walls or the floors – it is an uninsulated water cylinder. Heating water in an uninsulated cylinder is like trying to heat a room in which all the glass has been removed from the windows. In fact, an uninsulated cylinder wastes three-and-a-half times as much energy as an insulated one. Fitting a lagging jacket is one of the easiest, cheapest and most effective ways of saving energy. You should recoup the cost in a matter of months.

If you live in an average semi-detached house and have not insulated your attic, then 25 per cent of your heat is being wasted through the roof. If your doors and windows are not properly draught proofed, then you are also losing a considerable amount of heat. Experts have reckoned that the family heating bill can be cut by as much as 16 per cent by eliminating both internal and external draughts.

External walls are the biggest offenders when it comes to heat loss: they account for about 35 per cent. Dry-lining is one good way of insulating a wall. The value of double glazing in terms of insulation is relatively low on the list of insulating priorities, but if your windows are bad and you have to replace them anyway, then it makes sense to put in double glazing. Any insulation is better than no insulation, and remember that every bit of insulation translates into money saved in heating and energy costs.

Installing attic insulation is a job which is within the competence of almost everyone, but it is interesting to note that in a survey done some time ago 80 per cent of the people who buy the insulation material and bring it home are women. Who actually does the job didn't emerge from the survey, but these days a handy teenager could easily install it.

Moy Insulation is the largest manufacturer of insulation material in Ireland and they export 60 per cent of their products to the United Kingdom and Europe. They have a loft pack which is particularly well designed. It comes in handy lengths which slot between standard joists and can be easily cut with scissors or a Stanley knife to fit any odd spaces. If you want to find out how many packs you need to insulate your loft space, just measure the outside of your house and the width of your house in metres and multiply one by the other. Then divide the result by five. Each loft pack contains more than enough to insulate five square metres. The result is the number of packs required.

Insulation material comes compressed in a pack – the pieces expand when the pack is opened. I'm told you can fit eight packs into a Renault 5 car. It is relatively cheap to buy, so insulating your attic or topping up existing insulation need not be a highly expensive job. Under new building regulations – due to come into effect in late 1992 – it is expected that insulation requirements will go up from 100 mm in the attic to 150 mm, and from 40 mm in a cavity wall to at least 60 mm. Total underfloor insulation will be the norm. These requirements will apply not only to new houses, but also to extensions.

Insubordinate insulation:

Polystyrene in slab form is widely used as an insulating material. Polystyrene in bead form is used for stuffing cushions and bean bags and can quickly get out of hand, as I discovered some years ago.

I had been talking about bean bags to a friend in the business, saying what a useful form of seating they could provide in a family-room and that I would really love to make one from various bits of fabric I had lying around the house – a kind of multi-coloured bean bag. He took me at my word. Three weeks later, when I had completely forgotten all about bean bags, a large plastic sack of polystyrene beads were handed in at our front door. It was enormous, about five-foot high, and as round as a big barrel.

I left it in the hall until I could think of some place to put it. I didn't realise how tempting the beads were. A few tiny breaks in the bag were apparently irresistible to passing fingers, and very soon there was a gentle flutter of tiny white balls drifting into nearby rooms. My husband, meeting a mini-snowstorm as he came home from work, expressed himself rather violently. Hastily, I moved it upstairs to the study and tried sticking over the various perforations with Sellotape. Somehow there didn't seem to be time just then for making bean bags.

Polystyrene beads have a life and personality of their own. Even in the study they were determined to break free, with a little help along the way. When they began to look as if they might take over the study I banished them to the attic and promised myself I'd get a bigger, stronger bag and rehouse them. They rested in the attic for quite some time – or rather they didn't rest. Slowly and relentlessly they began to spread all over the assembled junk. There were stacks of old school books which I had sorted into subjects the previous autumn and neatly tied together, and which were now lying loose because different people looking for different books had undone the bundles and strewn them around the floor. Now they were covered with polystyrene beads, so were the boxes of old delft, the broken chairs, the old suitcases, the left-over pieces of carpet and the stacks of old magazines. Every time the attic door was opened, the beads came fluttering down the stairs; and every time I opened the door of the press under the stairs, they rained down on me like confetti.

One day before some visitors arrived, our youngest son, then aged eight, decided to be particularly helpful. He had been much taken with a pouffe case which had been given to us by some Egyptian friends. It was leather, beautifully coloured and tooled in gold, and I could quite understand his admiration. He just chose the wrong time to try to fill it with polystyrene beads, and since he didn't appreciate the necessity for an inner casing and wasn't quite sure how to tie up the opening anyway, the beads had a great time.

They tumbled over the attic floor in mounds, came down the stairs in drifts and floated gently into corners and crevices. Another son had a brilliant idea. The best way to clear them up, he decided, would be to push them all down the stairs so that they would be in one pile at the end. But polystyrene beads don't like being pushed, and when they get free they set out to enjoy themselves. By the time I discovered what had happened they were in the laundry, the central corridor, the bathroom, the dining-room and even the kitchen. And our German shepherd was covered in white dots.

Well how *do* you clear up thousands and thousands of wild polystyrene beads? With great difficulty, as I discovered. You put a clean bag into the vacuum cleaner, vacuum the beads up and then when the bag is full empty it all into a plastic bag and start again. This is fine in theory. But the beads appeared to be magnetised. A certain amount would go into the vacuum bag, then they would jam at the entrance. I spent two-and-a-half hours emptying partially filled bags into one black refuse sack before I reached the door of the attic. I vacuumed some more off the landing and the study and then gave up. I brushed what was left into the attic, found a key for the attic door and locked all the remaining chaos away. But eight years on, whenever I need access to the attic, I meet them again, in boxes and books, in cases and corners. And I never *did* get to make the bean bag.

• insurance claims

If you ever have to claim against an insurance company for serious damage to your house, a lot will depend upon how good a policy you have and how well you have read the small print. If you sit down in any one room in your house, say the kitchen or the dining-room, and add up the cost of replacing everything in it, the total figure might well surprise you. But total replacement will be what you want if, for instance, you have a bad fire.

If you have to make a claim, the insurance company will send you out a form, and after you have filled it, a loss adjustor to assess the damage. The insurance company doesn't have to help you fill in the form, nor is it the function of the loss adjustor to do so or of your insurance broker, if you have one. So a bit of professional help might well prove welcome.

You can, for example, go to a firm of loss assessors. Loss assessors offer a service to people hoping to get the best from their insurance policy. They act solely on behalf of the policy holder. They will carry out an in-depth survey of your losses and undertake a thorough examination of your insurance documents. They will formulate your building-damage claim and make a full inventory for loss of contents, negotiating all aspects of your claim with the appointed loss adjustor.

Loss Assessors:

Balcombes Ltd
21 Mespil Road
Dublin 4
☎ Dublin 607544

N. J. Carroll & Associates
226 Harold's Cross Road
Dublin 6 W
☎ Dublin 979432/966602

Cleary Callanan & Associates, Ltd
Huband House
16 Upper Mount Street
Dublin 2
☎ Dublin 768515

Cleary Callanan & Associates, Ltd
22–24 Prospect Hill
Eyre Square
Galway
☎ 091 64477

Skeffington Nolan
67 Merrion Square
Dublin 2
☎ Dublin 768588

• interior designers

If you want help with interior design or with decorating your home, you can call on the services of an interior designer. The Interior Decorators and Designers Association will direct you to one of their members in your own area. You can contact them at the following address.

The Interior Decorators and Designers Association
c/o Angela O'Connor
55 Shelbourne Road
Ballsbridge
Dublin 4
☎ Dublin 603733

If you want the name of an interior designer in Northern Ireland, you should contact the association at their Middlesex address.

Interior Decorators and Designers Association
Crest House
102–104 Church Road
Teddington
Middlesex TW11 8PY
☎ 081 9771105

I myself have been very impressed with the work done by **Nuala Roberts** of **Daydreams Interior Design** in Clonmel. She studied interior design in London and came back to set up business in Clonmel – from there she'll travel to any part of Ireland. She is full of sound, practical advice and has a brilliant eye for colour. You'll find her at 30 Parnell Street, Clonmel, ☎ 052 25851.

• ise waste disposals

F. E. Smith Electrical Ltd
3/5 Camden Place
Dublin 2
☎ Dublin 751702

• itt nova

Appliance Network Services Ltd
19 East Essex Street
Dublin 2
☎ Dublin 6795244/715528
(*Republic of Ireland*)

Teska Ltd
16 Cedarhurst Road
Newtownbreda
Belfast BT8 4RH
☎ 0232 644821
(*Northern Ireland*)

• jackson cookers

Ideal Service
Kylemore Park West
Ballyfermot
Dublin 10
☎ Dublin 6266720

jewellers

David Murray has a small jewellery shop at the top of Dawson Street in Dublin. The first time I visited him some years ago he had copies of old Irish Tara brooches on display. He had made them himself, he told me, meticulously copying the originals in the National Museum. But then he makes most of the jewellery in the shop himself, which is not as common as you might think. The majority of jewellery shops buy in their jewellery ready made. David said he liked copying old jewellery and showed me copies he had made of Victorian and Edwardian pieces he especially admired: delicate brooches and lovely rings. I remembered a drawing of a ring I had seen in an old book and asked if he could make me one. He could, he said, just bring in the drawing. Someday, I said, and put it 'on the long finger'.

More recently, I visited him again. I had noticed in the course of my peregrinations around other jewellery shops that old-fashioned watch chains had now become high fashion as necklaces. They were called Alberts. I recalled that I had one in an old box at home which had belonged to my grandfather and which I thought was made of copper. In fact, it was rose gold, which has a high element of copper in it.

'Bring it in', said David, 'and I'll polish it up for you.' But when I took it out and looked at it and brought it in, it was, in fact, too worn to repair. Parts of the links had almost disappeared – my grandfather had lived well into his eighties. It would be difficult to repair satisfactorily, said David. Soldering extra pieces on to the worn pieces didn't really work well. The best thing to do would be to melt it down and remake it. If we were going to melt it down, I said, I'd prefer to make it into something else. I didn't really see myself wearing an Albert. But I would like a copy of the ring I had seen in that old book, which is how I ended up with a ring I'd always wanted and enough left over to make rings for my three daughters – someday.

David started serving his time when he was fourteen and worked with a number of jewellers before he eventually set up on his own, fourteen years ago. One of the people who taught him most, he says, was a man called Peter Morgan who had originally come over from London to work with Wests in Grafton Street. 'He could make up all the old stuff, from tiaras to brooches, all hand done. I saw him working on pieces which took months to do. Another man called Willie Rabbitte taught me a lot about very fine work.'

He has continued learning all the time, he says. The jewellery business is a hard business to learn, and people are not always inclined to pass on the secrets of the trade. He showed me a sapphire-and-diamond engagement ring. 'These kind of rings are quite tricky to make. The formation has to be right; you have to do it properly. All those stones have to be put together all at once. It's an oval diamond-and-sapphire cluster, set with two little pear-shaped sapphires. There are three sapphires and eight diamonds altogether, and the stones are of very good quality. This kind of ring is very popular.'

At one time, big jewellery shops would employ tradesmen who specialised in different areas. As a one-man operation, David does a bit of everything. 'But I love working on the old stuff. I've just made a pattern for an old ring-setting with five sapphires set in diamonds. This is a master pattern, and it took me three days to make, but I can cast copies from that pattern now much more quickly. I'll probably cast about six copies altogether. These old settings never go out of fashion.'

Each year he makes probably twenty-five new patterns, and over the years he has built up quite a collection of patterns for rings, crosses, brooches, earrings and pendants. He likes difficult designs, but they must be designs which won't give trouble and about which customers will have no complaint. 'For example, you can see on that ring I have put a nice heavy band, about a 1.8 mm band. Many rings are made with a 1.3 mm band. If bands are made too light, you may save a bit of gold, but the ring won't be as good.' His brooches are particularly beautiful. Most of them are copies of old designs and are timeless in their elegance, set perhaps with small opals, amethysts or rubies and tiny diamonds. And as I've mentioned, he will make jewellery for people who want something special. 'They can bring me a picture out of a magazine, an illustration of something they like.' Some of the patterns he likes best have come to him in this way – through customers who wanted something specially made.

You will find **David Murray** at 25 Dawson Street, a few shops down from St Stephen's Green, on your left as you face Nassau Street, Dublin. You can also telephone David at ☎ Dublin 779228.

McDowells, 3 Upper O'Connell Street, Dublin, ☎ Dublin 744961/743184, is a very long-established jewellery house. As well as selling a wide range of jewellery, they also refashion and remount old pieces, especially rings. They can also make copies of old mounts.

David Ryan has taught people how to craft jewellery, makes jewellery by hand to order, and also repairs and restores work. He has three shops, all operating under the name of **Sterling Jewellers Ltd**, and you will find Sterling at the following addresses.

Sterling Jewellers Ltd
Unit 20, Crumlin Shopping Centre
Dublin 12
☎ Dublin 533444

Unit 7, Newbridge Shopping Centre
Newbridge
Co. Kildare
☎ 045 32863

Poplar Square
Naas
Co. Kildare
☎ 045 74044

Patrick Flood, Powerscourt Centre, Dublin 2, ☎ Dublin 6794256, is a designer goldsmith of good repute and standing. He designs and makes special pieces to order and also remodels old jewellery.

Declan Killen, 12 Fade Street, Dublin, ☎ Dublin 770829, restores and remodels jewellery of all kinds.

• jojo cable reels and accessories

Noel McCabe Distributors
Bluebell Industrial Estate
Dublin 12
☎ Dublin 502926

In Northern Ireland JoJo products are also serviced by Noel McCabe Distributors from Dublin.

• junkers water heating/ central heating

Beaver Engineering
Greenhills Road
Tallaght
Dublin 24
☎ Dublin 515211

• juno appliances

Electroservice
Long Mile Road
Dublin 12
☎ Dublin 518666

• jura irons

Noel McCabe Distributors
Bluebell Industrial Estate
Dublin 12
☎ Dublin 502926

• kal appliances

F. E. Smith Electrical Ltd
3/5 Camden Place
Dublin 2
☎ Dublin 751702

• kelvinator appliances

Ideal Service
Kylemore Park West
Ballyfermot
Dublin 10
☎ Dublin 6266720
(*Republic of Ireland*)

Robert Johnston
377b Antrim Road
Glengormley
Newtownabbey BT36 8EB
☎ 0232 342558
(*Northern Ireland*)

• kenwood

Kenwood's service agent is **Appliance Network Services Ltd**, 19 East Essex Street, Dublin 2, ☎ Dublin 6795244/715528.

There are a number of people who service Kenwood in Northern Ireland. Contact **Kenwood Ltd**, New Lane, Havant, Hampshire, PO9 2NH, ☎ 0705 476000, for the name and address of your nearest service agent.

• kenwood shavers

Gavins Shaver Centre
83 Lower Camden Street
Dublin 2
☎ Dublin 757109

• keys (see car keys)

kitchens

A new kitchen is a major event in the life of any house or any family. The kitchen, after all, is the core of the house, and a well-designed and fitted kitchen is often the favourite family-room, where people not only prepare food and cook it, but where they enjoy meals together, sit over a cup of tea or coffee and chat, or where they go when they first come home from school or work.

If you are planning to install a new kitchen with new units, appliances and perhaps floor covering, you will probably have been thinking about it for quite some time. You will be going to spend a substantial amount of money making it happen; therefore, it's very important that the job happens satisfactorily, and that you get the kitchen you want.

Before you go to look at any possible kitchens, sit down and ask yourself how much money you can afford to spend. You may have seen your dream kitchen in a glossy magazine, but if it costs £20,000, and you have only £5,000 to spend, then there's no point in setting your heart on it. Be realistic and set yourself limits. This will help you in the long run and it will also help the people who may be trying to sell you a kitchen. They are working from a manufacturer's price list, and when they know what you really intend to spend, it is easier for them to help you choose a kitchen within your price range. It will also be useful if you have some sort of plan of the kitchen you want. You can do this to scale on graph paper, mapping out a rough idea of how you see your kitchen taking shape. If you bring this along when you go to visit a kitchen centre, it will save both their time and your's and enable them to give you some initial idea of prices and possibilities.

Another alternative is to have a detailed plan for your kitchen drawn up by a professional kitchen consultant – someone who is not attached to *any* kitchen centre but works independently. If you have a detailed plan, which you can bring along to each centre you visit, then you can really compare between centres. If all the details and materials are specified, as they would be in this kind of plan, then there will be no arguments, and you will get a clear idea of the costs involved.

Jean Carroll has worked for the top kitchen people in Ireland and now is an independent kitchen consultant. If you are planning a new kitchen, she will come and see you, discuss your needs and your preferences, such as the colours you think you might like and the style of kitchen you favour, and then take all this information back to the drawing-board, producing a detailed plan and coloured visual of your kitchen. With this plan in hand, you can then visit a range of kitchen centres and show them precisely what you have envisaged.

This service, to my mind, has many advantages. First of all, you are going to get independent advice and information without any obligation to buy a particular brand of kitchen. Secondly, most kitchen centres will not hand out plans until the customer places an order, and rarely, I'm told, will they provide coloured perspective drawings. With these drawings you are in a much stronger position when you go out to buy. You can visit different kitchen centres, get quotations from each one and make direct comparisons.

The time to call Jean in is during the very early stages of planning, whether it is a house, an extension or a revamp of any old kitchen. You can write to **Jean Carroll** at 46 Philipsburgh Terrace, Marino, Dublin 3, or telephone her at ☎ Dublin 337580.

When you go to look at kitchens, don't just stand in the showroom and allow yourself to be dazzled by all those beautiful doors. It's what's behind the doors that is really important. Open them, pull out the drawers, examine the units. You want units which are really well built. You want shelves which will stand up to constant usage, with drawers which slide out easily. You want a kitchen that won't start to fall apart after eight or nine years. The base of the kitchen will almost always be made of chipboard, and you will need top-quality chipboard. You don't want your kitchen crumbling and flaking after a few years – this is known in the trade as a 'weetabix' kitchen.

You also want good, all-metal, rust-proof and fully adjustable hinges. Experts will tell you that you should look for protection against the effects of damp, because if there is water around, Murphy's Law says it will certainly find its way to the very places you don't want it to go. Good kitchen units have adjustable feet; they literally sit on stilts so that the material is protected in the event of leaking pipes. All units should carry an edging on the back to prevent dampness being absorbed. Worktops should be sealed all round.

Most people today are keen on built-in appliances. A white fridge or a white dishwasher can stand out in a coloured or wooden kitchen. The ultimate in the fitted kitchen is the completely integrated kitchen, with the same kind of doors on the appliances as you have on the units. It gives a much more finished look. Not all appliances, however, can be integrated, and it is very important that you don't try to build in an unsuitable appliance. You cannot build in a fridge which is designed to be free standing. If you build in a free-standing fridge, it will affect the cooling system, and the motor will have to cut on and off much more often; eventually it will wear out. If your dishwasher is going to be built in, then you must get one which is designed to be built in, otherwise you will have a gap between the worktop and the top of the dishwasher, which will simply collect dirt and dust.

One of the problems for the ordinary person buying a kitchen is that it can be difficult to assess the quality of the chipboard, the hinges and the fittings. This is why you should go to a good kitchen supplier. To a great extent, you have to rely on the reputation and integrity of the supplier, which brings us to the question of where to buy your kitchen. You can, for example, buy either from an established kitchen centre, your favourite local carpenter or cabinet maker, or direct from a salesman who calls at your home. There are very good arguments for buying locally and for buying from an established kitchen centre.

If you buy from a kitchen centre you can go to their showroom and see the kind of units you are thinking of purchasing. You can check up on the company's track record, because if it's good, they should be happy to give you the names and telephone numbers of satisfied customers. Ask about the tradesmen they employ to fit the kitchens; are they experienced in fitting their particular make of kitchen? Proper fitting is very important. Look for people who have been in the business for a reasonable period of time, people with a commitment to service and quality and with kitchen experience.

Buying from a local craftsman or cabinet maker can be very satisfactory. You will probably go to him first, because he has an established reputation in the area, and you will easily be able to see other kitchens he has built. Because he lives locally, he will be concerned about maintaining his good reputation and will be able to offer you good after-sales service.

You can also buy from a salesman who comes to your house. He may use high-pressure sales techniques to try to get you to commit yourself, he may be very pleasant, or he may be persuasive. But when you talk to him you may well find that he hasn't necessarily been in the kitchen business very long and that his knowledge of it is rather superficial. Essentially, his job is to sell, and if he doesn't sell then his pay cheque will suffer – which may be sad, but should not be sufficient reason to make you buy one of his kitchens.

There are some important 'don'ts' in kitchen buying. Don't be fooled by advertisements of special 'giveaway' offers and false discounts. Nothing is free – you only get what you pay for. Don't be seduced by the offer of a generous discount if you sign on the spot – this is a danger signal. It doesn't give you time to compare and shop around. Don't believe you're going to get a 'free' appliance with your kitchen, such as a 'free' oven or 'free' refrigerator. The real cost is probably hidden elsewhere in the price of your kitchen. Don't fall for a 'free fitting' offer either; somebody has to pay the joiners, electricians and plumbers who do the job, and the cost will probably be covered by you.

If you buy from the right people, they will give you good advice and good service. When I think of good kitchen people, I think of the following.

John Browne Interiors
Industrial Estate Mount Mahon
Abbeyfeale
Co. Limerick
☎ 068 31318/31434

Collier Kitchens Ltd
20 Crescent Place
Dublin 3
☎ Dublin 336870

Fitzsimons Fitted Kitchens
Laracor
Trim
Co. Meath
☎ 046 31192

(The vast majority of kitchens today are made with a chipboard carcass. **Fitzsimons Kitchens** make kitchens using both chipboard and MDF [medium density fibreboard], but they can also make you an entire kitchen of solid oak, if you want.)

Nolan Kitchens Ltd
Unit 50, Western Industrial Estate
Dublin 12
☎ Dublin 552621

Clive Nunn Furniture
Ballyduff Mill
Thomastown
Co. Kilkenny
☎ 056 58473
(solid-wood kitchen furniture, beautifully crafted)

Oakline Kitchens Ltd
8 Ranelagh
Dublin 6
☎ Dublin 977435/961276

Pat and Joe O'Connor
Dundrum Kitchen Centre
Apollo Building
Dundrum
Dublin 14
☎ Dublin 2980099

ORM Kitchens
Castlemartyr
Co. Cork
☎ 021 667100

ORM Kitchens
Drawbridge Street
Cork
☎ 021 270111

ORM Kitchens
60a Longmile Road
Dublin 12
☎ Dublin 506876

Ryan Furniture
Ballyloughane
Gorey
Co. Wexford
☎ 055 21585

Mark and Rosie Shortt
Siematic Kitchens
Erne Place
Holles Street
Dublin 2
☎ Dublin 2897390

At the time of going to press, efforts were still being made to set up an association of kitchen retailers in the Republic of Ireland. Such an association seems a good idea: it could set standards for the fitted-kitchen industry and the retail trade, and it would mean that the customer who bought from an association member had a guarantee of good standards and good service. The **Kitchen Specialists Association** provides this service in the United Kingdom and in Northern Ireland. People in Northern Ireland who would like to get a list of members in their immediate area can write to them.

Kitchen Specialists Association
PO Box 311
Worcester WR1 1DN
☎ 0905 726066

Kitchen gadgets and cooking aids:

Kitchen Complements, Chatham House, Chatham Street, Dublin 2, ☎ Dublin 770734, is a good place to go for cake tins in unusual shapes, moulds for sweets and chocolate making, and kitchen ware and cooking aids of all kinds.

The Ballymaloe Shop in Ballymaloe, Co. Cork, ☎ 021 652032, is run by Wendy Allen and is also a very good place to look for unusual equipment, as well as for unusual food. You'll find specialised moulds and shapes for tarts, tartlets, cakes and chocolates, and you'll see whisks, spoons and measures, icing bags and nozzles of all kinds, good pots and pans, and much else besides.

• krups shavers

Gavins Shaver Centre
83 Lower Camden Street
Dublin 2
☎ Dublin 757109

The **Krups Dublin Services Depot** for domestic appliances is found at the **Spare Parts Centre**, 9 North Frederick Street, Dublin 1, ☎ Dublin 726565. Otherwise post to Krups Engineering Ltd, Roxboro' Road, Limerick, ☎ 061 417844.

• lace, restored

Nellie O'Cleirigh (IPCRA)
38 Templemore Avenue
Rathgar
Dublin 6
☎ Dublin 976580

From June to September, Nellie O'Cleirigh is to be found at **Crafts and Curios**, Knightstown, Valentia Island, Co. Kerry.

lamps

I understand that there are quite a number of people around the country who have been given presents of beautiful table lamps by friends and relatives coming home from the United States, only to find that the lampholders are not suitable for our bulbs. In addition, the wiring is not safe for use on our voltages, and they can be very dangerous if not properly converted. Jack O'Brien in Galway has set up a workshop to convert these lamps to comply with safety regulations. He can also convert oil lamps and do repairs to lamps generally. You can write to **Jack O'Brien** at 37 Glenard Crescent, Salthill, Galway, or phone him at ☎ 091 22509.

Restoration of brass lamps:

The City Brass Shop
73/74 Francis Street
Dublin 8
☎ Dublin 542696

See also lighting

laundry

A word of advice about laundering and laundries. If you are bringing in a special piece to be laundered, something valuable or old, *tell* the people at the counter when you are leaving it behind. Show them particular marks and stains and let them examine it themselves. They will point out any areas where problems may occur. Some old materials can be very fragile, while some materials which have been exposed to sunshine for a number of years – velvet curtains, cushion covers – can become quite weak and may not be able to stand up to laundering. It is better that both you and the launderer are aware of any risks involved before, rather than after.

Laundries:

The Kelso Laundry, Rathmines Road, Dublin 6, ☎ Dublin 972089/978490, offers a particularly good service. They collect from houses all over Dublin city and county, as far south as Greystones, as far north as Skerries and as far west as Maynooth. They also offer a same-day shirt service. If you want your shirts cleaned in a hurry, you can leave them at the Kelso in Rathmines in the morning and get them back in the evening.

The Laundry and Dry Cleaning Shop
118–120 Lower Rathmines Road
Dublin 6
☎ Dublin 962467

365 North Circular Road
Dublin 7
☎ Dublin 308558

23 Sandymount Green
Dublin 4
☎ Dublin 683962

Yvonne Tuthill opened her first **Laundry and Dry Cleaning Shop** in the late eighties. Now she has three shops which offer four services – dry cleaning, a finished shirt service, a bag wash, and a no more iron service. The shops are open seven days a week, from 8.00 a.m. until 10.00 p.m. If you drop off your shirts one evening, you can collect them the next – they have a large number of gentlemen customers for this service. If you leave in your clothes for the bag wash, you get them back clean, dry and folded; you iron them yourself. Or you can wash your clothes yourself and leave them in for the 'no more iron' service: this costs £6 for fifteen items. The shops also offer a finished service for sheets and tablecloths. And they have a big self-service launderette business as well.

St Mary's Laundry
Stanhope Street
Dublin 7
☎ Dublin 777206
(another long-established Dublin laundry)

Celtic Linen Services
St Magdalens
Wexford
☎ 053 422244
(cater for domestic customers in the south-east)

In Northern Ireland all the following laundries do house collections.

Erne Laundry Ltd
Henry Street
Enniskillen BT74 7JX
☎ 0365 322137

Lilliput (Dunmurry) Ltd
Glenburn Road
Dunmurry
Belfast BT17 9AP
☎ 0232 618555

Standard Laundry
(Northern Ireland) Ltd
213/215 Donegall Avenue
Belfast BT12 6LU
☎ 0232 327295

Waveney Laundry Ltd
Clonavon
Ballymena BT43 5BJ
☎ 0266 42131

• le creuset

The Kitchenware Merchants Ltd
Robin Burns
19 Upper Cherryfield Avenue
Dublin 6
☎ Dublin 960329

Modref Ltd
Unit 1a, Portview Trade Centre
310 Newtownards Road
Belfast BT4 1HE
☎ 0232 456484
(*Northern Ireland*)

• leather

Bags and suitcases repaired:

Bag Repairs
Peter Cleary
11 Montague Lane, off Camden Street
Dublin 2

Inserts into old writing desks:

Paul Moynihan of **Bits and Pieces**, 78 Francis Street, Dublin 8 ☎ Dublin 541178, specialises in restoring old desks.

• leather embossing (see embossing)

• lec fridges and freezers

Appliance Network Services Ltd
19 East Essex Street
Dublin 2
☎ Dublin 6795244/715528
(*Republic of Ireland*)

• leisure appliances

Cookers:

Ideal Service
Kylemore Park West
Ballyfermot
Dublin 10
☎ Dublin 6266720

Showers:

Domestic Sales and Repair Services
219 Kingsway
Dunmurry
Belfast BT17 9SB
☎ 0232 301533

• lendi appliances

V. Leonard & Co. Ltd
44a Alliance Avenue
Belfast BT14 7LX
☎ 0232 745303

• lighting

Bob Bushell Ltd
2 Sir John Rogerson's Quay
Dublin 2
☎ Dublin 710044

Harkness Electrical Co.
150 Harold's Cross Road
Dublin 6
☎ Dublin 977937

Lighting World
121–122 James's Street
Dublin 8
☎ Dublin 717788

Hicken Lighting
Wicklow Street, Talbot Street and Bridge Street
Dublin
☎ Dublin 777882
(shades made to order, from an extensive selection in the shops or from your own fabric)

Christopher Wray's Lighting Shop, 43–44 Frances Street, Dublin 8, ☎ Dublin 537222, carries an enormous range of fittings of all kinds, specialising in reproductions of old lighting fittings from Regency lamps to grand hotel pendant lights, elaborate lanterns, crystal chandeliers, billiard lamps on brass hangings, old-style brass ceiling fans with light fittings, and Chinese porcelain vase lamps. There are highly decorative Tiffany-style lamps here, each lamp individually handmade in the style and construction methods originally created by Louis Comfort Tiffany.

Of particular interest to many people must be the fact that the shop also does oil lamps, again reproductions of original and elegant old designs. And not only do they sell new oil lamps, they also sell parts for old lamps – globes or mantles, chimneys, burners and wicks.

Christopher Wray's have recently opened in Northern Ireland, and you will find them at 42 Bedford Street, Belfast BT1, ☎ 0232 231140.

Paul Moynihan in **Bits and Pieces**, 78 Francis Street, Dublin 8, ☎ Dublin 541178, has a good range of genuine old lights, including period ceiling lights and wall lights.

• looking glass (see mirrors)

• mcculloch saws

Noel McCabe Distributors
Bluebell Industrial Estate
Dublin 12
☎ Dublin 502926

In Northern Ireland service is also carried out by Noel McCabe Distributors in Dublin.

• magimix

MX Electrical
49 South William Street
Dublin 2
☎ Dublin 6792398

• maps (old), repaired and restored

David Skinner (IPCRA)
Paper Conservation Studio
Celbridge Mill, Celbridge
Co. Kildare
☎ Dublin 6272913

• mellerware small appliances

Dimpco Ltd
Airport Road
Cloghran
Dublin 9
☎ Dublin 8428222

To find the name of your nearest service person in Northern Ireland, contact Brownbrook Distributors.

Brownbrook Distributors Ltd
Unit 24, Seagoe Industrial Estate
Portadown
Co Armagh BT63 5TH
☎ 0762 337317

microwaves

More and more people today are buying microwave ovens. Indeed, the microwave oven could be called the biggest success story in domestic appliance sales over the last decade. And there is no doubt that a microwave oven can be a very useful addition to any kitchen.

A microwave cooks fish superbly, vegetables beautifully, sauces painlessly and scrambled eggs excellently. It is good for people on diets because you can cook with the minimum of fat and is excellent at reheating food. If you have a large family coming in at different times, you can cook one dinner, plate it up, and let people heat their own dinner as they come in – it won't taste reheated, it will taste as though it has just been cooked.

A microwave oven saves time and simplifies a number of small jobs in the kitchen. You can make porridge in the dish it is going to be served in – it's ready in about two minutes, and you have no dirty saucepan to wash. You can melt a whole block of jelly in seconds so that you can add cold water to it and the jelly will set in no time. You can make cocoa or drinking chocolate in a mug – again, no dirty saucepans.

The microwave is also invaluable for defrosting food: the lasagne you made a month ago, the bread you forgot to take out of the freezer last night, or the butter that is too hard to spread. I find I use it more for all these smaller chores than for cooking a big meal, but then I can be cooking for nine or ten at a time. The more food you put into the microwave, the longer it is going to take to cook it, and you eventually reach a point where you might as well use a conventional oven. Baked potatoes for ten, for instance, would not be a sensible proposition. But a full meal for two would be more than feasible.

I see the microwave oven as complementary to a conventional oven, not *replacing* it. To expect a microwave oven to do all the cooking for a family would be unreasonable. On the other hand, for a couple just married and setting up house, a microwave oven would serve them well as a beginning; however, I personally would always want a traditional oven as well. You can get combination ovens, but I think it is much better to use the microwave oven for doing what it does so efficiently, instead of trying to make it do the work of an ordinary oven as well. I think combination ovens are hard to keep clean, especially when they have a grill element. This is only my opinion; there will be those who swear by them.

I always tell anybody buying a microwave oven to get one with a stainless-steel interior. It's so much easier to clean; if you put a bowl of hot water in it and let it boil, you can wipe the surfaces clean, and if you put a piece of lemon in the water, it will smell even fresher.

The wattage of microwave ovens varies. The higher the wattage, the faster the cooking. The majority of ovens on the market range between 600 and 700 watts, though there are ovens with higher outputs. On very basic ovens you may only get three levels of power: high, medium and low; on other more sophisticated models you can get variable power control, a temperature control, a memory facility and an auto-timer.

Some models have a turn-table, others may have rotating antennae instead. Opinions differ about which is best. Some say that a rotating turn-table cooks better, but it means you can only use a dish which will fit on the table and be able to rotate. An oven with a rotating antenna is designed to distribute the microwaves throughout the cavity, so you can cook bigger dishes in it, though you should turn them manually from time to time or you may get uneven cooking. But you can get ovens which have both a stirrer and a turn-table, which means you can use the turn-table for smaller dishes and the stirrer for dishes which haven't room to revolve.

Two additional points: some ovens have manual controls, some have digital controls. Personally, I prefer the digital controls. I think it makes it easier to time things precisely. Secondly, most people don't really need an enormous microwave oven: a one-cubic-foot capacity is more than adequate for the needs of most families.

Microwave ovens come at a wide range of price. You have to decide what you are going to use it for, how much you are going to use it, and buy accordingly. Do you just want it to reheat and defrost? In that case, a basic model will serve your needs. Or do you want it to cook dishes for you right across the board? Do you want a timer, a memory? The more sophisticated you go, the higher the price.

Repairs:

If you have a problem with your microwave, you'll find the service agent listed alphabetically under the microwave's brand name.

• miele appliances

Miele Ireland
Beside the Red Cow Inn
Wilton House
Naas Road
Dublin 22
☎ Dublin 504024
(*Republic of Ireland*)

Kee (Hospital) Services
46 Bradbury Place
Belfast BT7 1RU
☎ 0232 322916
(Northern Ireland)

• mira showers

Modern Plant Ltd
Otter House
Naas Road
Clondalkin
Dublin 22
☎ Dublin 591344
(*Republic of Ireland*)

W. H. Leech & Son Ltd
Unit 3, 34 Montgomery Road
Belfast BT6 9HL
☎ 0232 401909
(*Northern Ireland*)

• mirrors/frames, restored and gilded

Cresten Doherty
45 Grange Court
Rathfarnham
Dublin 14
☎ Dublin 941639

Cresten Doherty was born in India, educated in England and studied at art college in Kent , where she left school at sixteen. From art college she went into the Royal Air Force, getting a commission at the very young age of eighteen. She was a pilot officer when she met an Irish flight-lieutenant, then married him and spent the next thirteen years travelling around the Mediterranean wherever her husband was posted. She first started doing picture-frame restoration because her mother was restoring for dealers in the west of England. By nature a perfectionist, she set out to learn everything she could about the art. Today she restores picture frames for many leading antique dealers.

A. C. Taylor, Upper Sandwith Street, Dublin 2, ☎ Dublin 765441, destain and resilver old mirrors. They do bevelling and brilliant cutting in straight lines and in shapes. They also tint mirrors and sandblast patterns and designs on glass. If you have had any accidents with glass, chances are they'll be able to do something for you. They repair cut -crystal drinking glasses, though this does not mean that they can repair a glass which has shattered into pieces; however, if you have a glass with a chip out of the rim, they can grind it down and make it look as good as new.

• moelle hair dryers

Noel McCabe Distributors
Bluebell Industrial Estate
Dublin 12
☎ Dublin 502926

Noel McCabe Distributors also look after servicing in Northern Ireland.

• moffat appliances

Electroservice
Long Mile Road
Dublin 12
☎ Dublin 518666
(Republic of Ireland)

Electrolux Tricity Bendix Service
Unit 3, Edenderry Industrial Estate
326 Crumlin Road
Belfast BT14 7EE
☎ 0232 746591
(Northern Ireland)

• morphy richards appliances

Dimpco Ltd
Airport Road
Cloghran
Dublin 9
☎ Dublin 8428222

In Northern Ireland contact Brownbrook Distributors to find the name of your nearest service agent.

Brownbrook Distributors Ltd
Unit 24, Seagoe Industrial Estate
Portadown
Co. Armagh BT63 5TH
☎ 0762 337317

• moulinex appliances

Beaumark Service Company
Sunbury Industrial Estate
Walkinstown
Dublin 12
☎ Dublin 504620

For service in Northern Ireland, the best thing to do is to contact Moulinex/Swan Holdings in Birmingham.

Moulinex/Swan Holdings Ltd
Moulinex Swan House
Albion Street
Birmingham B1 3DL
☎ 021 2001313/2001212

• name tapes

School uniforms cost money, quite a lot of money, and replacing a lost garment can be an expensive business. One way of cutting down on losses is to have clothes clearly marked. **Catherine Sargent** specialises in the business of making name tapes for clothes in high-quality fray-proof cotton, which can be either ironed directly on to the cloth or sewn on, if you prefer. They can be supplied with the name of the school and the owner clearly printed in indelible ink, and the tapes are highly resistant to dry cleaning and laundry washing. The tapes cost £1 for ten, £2 for twenty-five plus thirty pence for postage and packaging. You can write to **Catherine Sargent** at **Anim Tapes**, PO Box 1641, Dublin 13, or you can telephone her at Dublin ☎ 846221 1.

• neff cookers

Appliance Care
Unit 4, Ballymount Drive
Ballymount Industrial Estate
Walkinstown
Dublin 12
☎ Dublin 502655
(*Republic of Ireland*)

Euro Serv (Ireland) Ltd
66 Dows Road
Drumbo
Belfast BT8 8LB
☎ 0232 826446
(*Northern Ireland*)

• new world

Gas cookers:

There is a big network of service agents for cookers using Calor Kosangas, and any dealer stockist will have a list. If you can't find one, contact the following.

Calor Kosangas
Long Mile Road
Dublin 12
☎ Dublin 505000

If your cooker is run on Flogas Ergas, contact Flogas.

Flogas Ergas
Dublin Road
Drogheda
Co Louth
☎ 041 31041

If it is run on natural gas, contact your local gas company.

In Northern Ireland contact the following companies.

Calor Gas (Northern Ireland) Ltd
Airport Road West
Sydenham
Belfast BT3 9EE
☎ 0232 458466
(cookers using Calor Kosangas)

Flogas (Northern Ireland) Ltd
Airport Road West
Belfast BT3 9ED
☎ 0232 732611
(cookers using Flogas Ergas)

Hobs:

Euro Serv (Ireland) Ltd
66 Dows Road
Drumbo
Belfast BT8 8LH
☎ 0232 826446

• newhome sewing machines

Sew-Knit Machine Centre
26 Bridge Street
Lisburn BT28 1XY
☎ 0846 601200

• nilko (fakir/nilco) vacuum cleaners and polishers

Noel McCabe Distributors
Bluebell Industrial Estate
Dublin 12
☎ Dublin 502926

Noel McCabe also services Northern Ireland.

• normende tvs and videos

Consumer Electronics
Unit 16, Western Parkway
Business Centre
Lower Ballymount Road
Dublin 12
☎ Dublin 500144
(*Republic of Ireland*)

Tele Video Services
6 Kilwee Industrial Estate
Dunmurry BT17 0HQ
☎ 0232 617222
(*Northern Ireland*)

• nova (see itt nova)

• novum appliances

Bluebell Appliance Service Ltd
Naas Road
Dublin 12
☎ Dublin 783955/508455

• nyda appliances

Electroservice
Long Mile Road
Dublin 12
☎ Dublin 518666

• oil paintings, restored

James A. Gorry (IPCRA)
20 Molesworth Street
Dublin 2
☎ Dublin 6795319

Jimmy Gorry is one of the best-known restorers of paintings in Ireland. His grandfather and his father before him were also master restorers. His son is now the fourth generation, and the fourth James Gorry, in the business.

John Dawson-Evans
(IPCRA)
Farrendeelion
Ballina
Co. Mayo

Stella Harte (IPCRA)
94 Martin's Row
Chapelizod
Co. Dublin
☎ Dublin 6266127

Roland Hulme-Beaman
(IPCRA)
30 Leeson Park Avenue
Ranelagh
Dublin 6
☎ Dublin 604850

Mary McGrath (IPCRA)
The Mill
Celbridge
Co. Kildare
☎ Dublin 6273419

Teresa Meyler (IPCRA)
15 Primrose Street
Dublin 7
☎ Dublin 306796

Andrew O'Connor
19 Upper Lad Lane
Dublin 2

In Northern Ireland contact the following restorers.

Alan Campell (IPCRA)
Hillview
Bigh Lane
Tempo
Co. Fermanagh
☎ 036 554357

Lynn Stinson (IPCRA)
6 Darragh
Whiterock
Killinchy
Co. Down
☎ 0238 541734

• opus showers

Ideal Service
Kylemore Park West
Ballyfermot
Dublin 10
☎ Dublin 6266720
(*Republic of Ireland*)

Domestic Sales and Repairs Ltd
219 Kingsway
Dunmurry
Belfast BT17 9SB
☎ 0232 301533
(*Northern Ireland*)

• paint

For useful advice on painting and decorating, talk to **Denis O'Driscoll** in **DOD Ltd,** 62 Mary Street, Dublin 1, ☎ Dublin 730699. Denis has a spectrophotometer, which is a computer that can match fabrics, carpets or tiles exactly; it lists the formulation of the paint, which is then fed into another machine to give you precisely the shade you require.

You might also contact **Joe Coghlan** of **MRCB** 12-13 Cornmarket, Dublin 8, ☎ Dublin 6798755. Joe Coghlan wrote the *Advanced Manual for Painting and Wallpapering*, which was published by the Irish Hardware Association for the use of senior staff in the hardware trade. He is a fund of knowledge and experience, and anybody who would like to know the right and wrong way to go about doing a decorating job will learn a lot from him. Joe is open six days a week and through lunchtime, from 8.00 a.m. to 5.30 p.m.

• panasonic hi-fi and video equipment

Panasonic Smurfit Ireland Ltd
88 Dublin Industrial Estate
Dublin 11
☎ Dublin 307622
(*Republic of Ireland*)

Wilmor & Company
Morton House
10 Lorne Street
Belfast BT9 7DU
☎ 0232 381521
(*Northern Ireland*)

• paraglow heaters

J. C. Distribution Ltd
Clonard Road
Dublin 12
☎ Dublin 902811

• parkinson cowan gas cookers

There is a big network of service agents around the country for cookers run on Calor Kosangas. Any dealer stockist will have a list. If you can't find one, contact **Calor Kosangas**, Long Mile Road, Dublin 12, ☎ Dublin 505000.

If your cooker is run on Flogas Ergas, contact **Flogas Ergas**, Dublin Road, Drogheda, Co. Louth, ☎ 041 31041.

If it is run on natural gas, contact your local natural gas company.

In Northern Ireland contact **Calor Gas (Northern Ireland) Ltd**, Airport Road West, Sydenham, Belfast BT3 9EE ☎ 0232 458466, if your cooker is run on Calor Kosangas.

If it is run on Flogas Ergas, contact **Flogas (Northern Ireland) Ltd**, Airport Road West, Belfast BT3 9ED, ☎ 0232 732611.

parties and party accessories

If you are having a party and you want to hire out crockery, cutlery, glassware, furniture, cooling equipment or linen, you might like to go to **Sam Party Hire** for help and assistance. If there is any unusual or special equipment they haven't stocked and you want, they will almost certainly know where to get it. Their stock covers for 5,000 people at any one time, so unless you are planning a party with hundreds of people, they can usually supply you with everything within a few days' notice. The person to talk to is **Marion Webster**, and she is at **Sam Party Hire**, Unit 601, Chestnut Road, Western Industrial Estate, Naas Road, Dublin. You can telephone her at ☎ Dublin 509922.

• pest control

A-Verminex
Noel Buggy
19 Rosemount Road
Dublin 7
☎ Dublin 305996/8680996

Noel Buggy is a man who specialises in dealing with pests and parasites. These can be wasps, ants or cock-roaches, rats, mice or woodlice, earwiggs, moths or fleas, or beetles of one kind or another – indeed, any unwanted insects in your house. Noel deals with them with zest and despatch.

• pewter repairs

Sean Carroll & Sons Ltd
Granary Hall
18 Rutland Street
Cork
☎ 021 311757

Regal Silver
Unit 3, IDA Centre
The Coombe
Dublin 8
☎ Dublin 532646

• philco home laundry

K. T. Distributors
Unit 2, Baloo Crescent
Balloo Industrial Estate
Bangor
Co. Down BT19 2YX
☎ 0247 270130

• philips

Washing machines, tumble dryers, fridges, freezers, microwaves, oven hobs and hoods, and dishwashers:

Philips and Whirlpool Major Appliances
Unit 4, Allied Industrial Estate
Kylemore Road
Dublin 10
☎ Dublin 6231013

In Northern Ireland contact the following addresses.

Euro Serv (Ireland) Ltd
66 Dows Road
Drumbo
Belfast BT8 8LH
☎ 0232 826446

Domestic Sales and Repair Services Ltd
219 Kingsway
Dunmurry
Belfast BT17 9SB
☎ 0232 301533

Small appliances:

Philips Electronics (Ireland) Ltd
Newstead
Clonskeagh
Dublin 14
☎ Dublin 640264
(*Republic of Ireland*)

At Philips Electronics, Adrienne Ryan will provide you with the name of your nearest service dealer.

Euro Serv (Ireland) Ltd
66 Dows Road
Drumbo
Belfast BT8 8LB
☎ 0232 826446
(*Northern Ireland*)

TVs, audio and video equipment:

Philips Electronics (Ireland) Ltd
Newstead
Clonskeagh
Dublin 14
☎ Dublin 640171/670174
(*Republic of Ireland*)

At Philips Electronics, Deirdre McInerney will give you the name of your nearest service dealer.

V. Leonard & Co. Ltd
44a Alliance Avenue
Belfast BT14 7LX
☎ 0232 749326
(*Northern Ireland*)

• philishave shavers

Gavins Shaver Centre
83 Lower Camden Street
Dublin 2
☎ Dublin 757109

Domestic Sales and Repair Services Ltd
219 Kingsway
Dunmurry
Belfast BT17 9SB
☎ 0232 301533

• photographs

David Davidson, Edwin Davidson (IPCRA)
277 Upper Kilmacud Road
Dublin 14
☎ Dublin 2986175

The Davidsons, father and son, restore old photographs and make modern versions of old photographs using old processes.

• picture frames (see mirrors/frames)

• pifco/salton appliances

Appliance Network Services Ltd
19 East Essex Street
Dublin 2
Dublin 6795244/715528

In Northern Ireland contact the following.

Teska Ltd
16 Cedarhurst Road
Newtownbreda
Belfast BT8 4RH
☎ 0232 644821

• pifco shavers

Gavins Shaver Centre
83 Lower Camden Street
Dublin 2
☎ Dublin 757109

• pine furniture

Pine furniture has been very popular for a considerable number of years and is available around the country in varying qualities of design and craftmanship and in a range of prices. Anybody who plans to buy should shop around for good quality and good finish. Places and people you could visit include the following.

Steve and Aoife Elster of **Heartwood**, 28 Market Arcade, South Great George's Street, Dublin, ☎ Dublin 6799628, are geophysicists who have become makers of furniture. They met working in the oil industry in the UK. The oil industry, says Aoife, 'is full of people who want to get out of it and do something else. We decided we wanted to run our own business. Steve had always been good with his hands and liked working with wood. We decided to come back to Ireland and start making furniture.'

They make pine bedroom furniture, including beds with

drawers underneath, and more recently have begun crafting kitchen furniture in Stradbally, Co. Laois. If you live in the Dublin area, you can visit them in the Market Arcade; if you live outside Dublin, visit them at The Green, Stradbally, ☎ 0502 25285.

Cody's of 53 Capel Street, Dublin, ☎ Dublin 731181, stock an excellent range of pine furniture – good-looking kitchen and dining-room furniture and first-class bedroom furniture. They have pine beds with storage drawers underneath: the drawers roll out easily on castors and are ideal for children's rooms where space is at a premium. These are made by Duckers in the UK. Cody's also stock handsome pine bedroom furniture made by Erinwood in Co. Antrim. The range includes wardrobes, chests of drawers, dressing tables, bedside tables and blanket boxes, all made to a very high standard of craftmanship. You can telephone Cody's at ☎ Dublin 731181.

Erinwood furniture, which is made in Co. Antrim, is available in the Creations shops in Northern Ireland. The addresses are listed below.

Creations
Market Square
Lisburn
Co. Antrim BT28 1AG
☎ 0846 666210

29 Great Victoria Street
Belfast BT2 7AD
☎ 0232 323197

33 Mill Street
Ballymena BT43 5AA
☎ 0266 49787

• plaster work

Seamus O'hEocha (IPCRA)
87 Fr Griffin Road
Galway
☎ 091 65286

Denis Clancy (IPCRA)
31 Forrest Hills
Rathcoole
Co. Dublin
☎ Dublin 580439

• pleating

French Pleating Co.
12a Rear Wexford Street
Dublin 2
☎ Dublin 784662

French Pleating have, in their time, pleated everything from christening robes to shrouds. Mostly, they pleat materials for children's and ladies wear, for wedding dresses and confirmation dresses, and for dance dresses.

• plumbing fittings

J. L. Smallman
1 Bachelor's Way
off Bachelor's Walk
Dublin 1
☎ Dublin 732510

pots and pans

Every kitchen and every cook needs cookware – good cookware. Using the right kind of pot or pan for the job is very important. Today there is a wide range of cookware on the market, and it can sometimes be difficult to decide which kind to buy. Some of the really good pots and pans can seem very expensive. On the other hand, if you buy a good set of pots and pans, knowing that you will probably use them for many years, even a lifetime, you have made a worthwhile investment.

A good saucepan or pot is something you could well be using every day. Certainly, a good proportion of the cookware in the kitchen will be used most days in any house. Only you know the kind of cooking you do, the kind of meals you most commonly prepare, so only you can choose the kind of saucepans you need. Most people probably require a mix of pots, pans and casseroles, some to use on the hob, some to put in the oven and some suitable for microwave use.

One of the basic requirements of any cooking utensil is that it distribute heat evenly, wherever it is cooking. Some materials conduct heat more quickly and more efficiently than others. Silver (yes, a number of people used to cook in silver saucepans, and silver chafing dishes are still in use), is the most efficient. Then comes copper, aluminium, cast iron, stainless steel, earthenware, porcelain and glass. The heavier the pot and the thicker the bottom, the more evenly the heat will be conducted. Of course, the heavier and thicker the bottom, the less likely it is to buckle. A saucepan with a buckled bottom will distribute heat unevenly. You'll get hot spots – points where food may stick and burn – especially if you are cooking on an electric plate or a solid-fuel stove. With gas, the problem may not be so noticeable.

Copper was one of the first metals to be used in cooking utensils and is, next to silver, the very best heat conductor. Copper looks beautiful as well as cooks beautifully, and it is a pleasure to use. But it is only worth buying the really good heavy-weight copper, and pots and pans in top-quality copper can be very expensive indeed. Copper also needs care. You must be prepared to spend time keeping it clean and shiny, and you should use only a wooden or plastic spoon, never a metal tool, or you can damage the special lining. But really good copperware is something you can pass on to your children – and some of the very best is made here in Ireland by **Castle Brand,** down in Nenagh, Co. Tipperary.

Cast iron has been used in kitchen utensils and cookware for centuries. It is said to have been employed first in China for water kettles and rice bowls. It was certainly the common material in kitchen utensils in Europe and America for hundreds of years. Cast iron conducts heat evenly, retains heat and can withstand most normal kitchen temperatures. And, while some utensils can be bought today in plain cast iron without any special finish, enamelled cast iron is the most popular. For one thing, it is easier to maintain. Un-enamelled cast iron does require a certain amount of care. It has to be kept scrupulously clean and dried thoroughly or it will rust. If food burns on it and sticks, it has to be reseasoned. (Wash the pan, dry it really well, rub it with oil, heat it up gently, wipe it with kitchen paper and a little salt, re-oil it and use.)

Stainless steel cookware has become very popular in recent years, and many people who used aluminium saucepans all their lives have turned over to stainless steel because of the stories about aluminium and Altzheimer's disease. Stainless steel is very strong, is not easily dented, resists corrosion and keeps its nice, shiny finish with the minimum of care. If you do have an accident with it and it gets badly burned, it can more easily be restored than most other saucepans. You need to look for a stainless-steel pot with a good, strong bottom to ensure even heat conduction. There are some excellent stainless-steel pots on the market nowadays, and it is well worth shopping around – prices can vary considerably from store to store.

Apart from the various metals, glass, ceramics and earthenware are also used in cookware. Generally, **glass** has a rather low and uneven heat conductivity, but it retains heat well, so it's good in the oven. Also, glass isn't porous, so it won't rust. On the other hand, if it gets scratched, or if you scrub it too hard with an abrasive or even with a coarse metal pad, it becomes more difficult to clean, because food tends to stick in the scratches.

The very first cooking vessels were made of **clay**, and down the centuries the use of clay has been developed and refined until today it is available in a wide range of oven tableware. **Stoneware** is a ceramic that has been fired at a higher temperature than earthenware and is particularly good for oven use. It's tougher than earthenware and will not absorb flavours or odours.

Last, but not least, is **aluminium** cookware, with which all of us are familiar. Aluminium utensils come in a wide variety of grades, from the very thinnest, right up to thick, quarter-inch (half-a-centimetre) aluminium in top-quality saucepans. Again, you should only buy the best. Good aluminium pots should be heavy and thick. Aluminium is a good conductor of heat, but if your pot is very thin, it will be more inclined to buckle, and the food will be more likely to stick. Aluminium doesn't rust, but it can get pitted by alkalis and a few acids.

• powerpoint appliances

Ideal Service
Kylemore Park West
Ballyfermot
Dublin 10
☎ Dublin 6266720

• pressure cooker parts

Spare Parts Centre
8 North Frederick Street
Dublin 1
☎ Dublin 726565

The Spare Parts Centre has parts for Tower, Presto, Prestige, Seb and Moulinex pressure cookers. Lid seals, safety valves, handles and indicator weights are in stock all the time. Other parts can be obtained within a few days.

• prestige kitchenware

MX Electrical
49 South William Street,
Dublin 2
☎ Dublin 6792398

• prints, repaired and restored

Susan Corr (IPCRA)
Paper Conservation Studio
48 Woodley Park
Dundrum
Dublin
☎ Dublin 2987661

Pat McBride (IPCRA)
Paper Conservation Studio
IDA Tower Complex
Pearse Street
Dublin 2
☎ Dublin 775655

David Skinner (IPCRA)
Paper Conservation Studio
Celbridge Mill
Celbridge
Co. Kildare
☎ Dublin 6272913

• rattan cane (for repairing furniture)

Singer Sewing and Craft Centre
54 Capel Street
Dublin 1
☎ Dublin 730623

• recycling

For advice on recycling, contact the **Environment Information Service (ENFO)**, 17 Andrew Street, Dublin 2, ☎ Dublin 6793144. They will send you, free of charge, leaflets on recycling glass, plastics, paper, metals and oil, and a list of addresses and collection centres.

• redring showers

GEC Distributors
15 Hendrick Street
Dublin 7
☎ Dublin 775413
(Republic of Ireland)

Domestic Sales and Repair Services
219 Kingsway
Dunmurry
Belfast BT17 9SB
☎ 0232 301533
(Northern Ireland)

• refrigerators

If you have a problem with your refrigerator, you'll find the service agent listed alphabetically under the brand name.

• regal fires

Brownbrook Distributors Ltd
Unit 24, Seagoe Industrial Estate
Portadown
Co. Armagh BT63 5TH
☎ 0762 337317

• remington shavers

Gavins Shaver Centre
83 Lower Camden Street
Dublin 2
☎ Dublin 757109

• roofers

The Construction Industry Federation can supply you with a list of roofing contractors. Write to **Federation House,** Canal Road, Dublin 6, or phone them at ☎ Dublin 977487.

• rotalux hair dryers and shoe polishers

Noel McCabe Distributors
Bluebell Industrial Estate
Dublin 12
☎ Dublin 502926

Domestic Sales and Repair Services
219 Kingsway
Dunmurry
Belfast BT17 9SB
☎ 0232 301533

• rowenta appliances

Appliance Network Services Ltd
19 Essex Street
Dublin 2
☎ Dublin 715528/6795244

There are a number of service agents for Rowenta in Northern Ireland. Contact **Customer Services**, Unit 4, Redbourne Park, Brackmills Industrial Estate, Northampton, ☎ 0604 760291, for the name of your nearest agent.

• russell hobbs

Beaumark Service Company
Sunbury Industrial Estate
Walkinstown
Dublin 12
☎ Dublin 504620

In Northern Ireland contact the following distributors.

Teska Ltd
16 Cedarhurst Road
Newtownbreda
Belfast BT8 4RH
☎ 0232 644821

salora tvs and videos

Nokia Smurfit
Unit 31, Western Parkway
Business Centre
Lower Ballymount Road
Dublin 12
☎ Dublin 568333

Nokia Smurfit will supply you with the name of your nearest serviceman.

For the name of your nearest service dealer in Northern Ireland, contact Nokia Consumer Electronics.

Nokia Consumer Electronics
Bridgemead Close
Westmead
Swindon SN5 7YG
☎ 0793 512939

salton appliances

Appliance Network Services Ltd
19 East Essex Street
Dublin 2
☎ Dublin 6795244/715528

In Northern Ireland contact the following addresses.

Teska Ltd
16 Cedarhurst Road
Newtownbreda
Belfast BT8 4RH
☎ 0232 644821

Domestic Sales and Repair Services
219 Kingsway
Dunmurry
Belfast BT17 9SB
☎ 0232 301533

sam hire

There are many companies which hire out equipment, but I have found **Sam Hire** particularly good. They tell you *everything* you need to know about the machine you are hiring, and they carefully check every machine when it comes back and before it goes out again. They're helpful and very patient, even with people like me who need basic instructions spelt out for them. They now have branches all over Ireland, as well as in Dublin.

Dublin:

Sam Hire
Near the Red Cow Inn
Naas Road
Dublin 22
☎ Dublin 593716

Dargle Centre
Castle Street
Bray
Co. Dublin
☎ Dublin 2825111

Coolmine Industrial Estate
Clonsilla
Dublin 15
☎ Dublin 8217022

11 Maypark
Malahide Road
Dublin 5
☎ Dublin 311388

Galway:

Sam Hire
Corbett Commercial Centre
Wellpark
Galway
☎ 091 53959

Limerick:

Sam Hire
Blackboy Pike
Mulgrave Street
Limerick
☎ 061 416766

Sligo:

Sam Hire
Pirnhill Road
Sligo
☎ 071 70370

Waterford:

Sam Hire
Tramore Road
Waterford
☎ 051 72314

Westmeath:

Sam Hire
Unit 4, Diskin Commercial Centre
Golden Pond
Athlone, Co. Westmeath
☎ 0902 74711

Wexford:

Sam Hire
Ferrycarrig Road Park
Wexford
☎ 053 45444

• samsung

Satellite systems, cameras and watches:

Photopak
204 Naas Road
Dublin 12
☎ Dublin 520500

TVs and videos:

Hi-Tech Electronics
Unit 20
Cookstown Enterprise Park
Old Belgarde Road
Tallaght
Dublin 24
☎ Dublin 512580/526234

Microwave ovens:

Crystal Clear TV Service
12a Terenure Road
Dublin 6
☎ Dublin 904041

In Northern Ireland Samsung appliances and equipment are looked after by Tele Video Services.

Tele Video Services
6 Kilwee Industrial Estate
Dunmurry BT17 OHQ
☎ 0232 617222

sanyo

TVs, videos, hi-fi equipment and microwaves:

Sanyo
Unit 41, Western Parkway
Business Centre
Ballymount Road
Dublin
☎ Dublin 503400

Microwaves outside the Dublin area:

Ideal Service
Kylemore Park West
Ballyfermot
Dublin 10
☎ Dublin 6266720

In Northern Ireland Craigavon TV Service will look after most Sanyo equipment.

Craigavon TV Service
17 Logan Drive
Lurgan
Craigavon BT66 8DA
☎ 0762 326119/322505

For microwave oven servicing, contact Coachhouse Foods.

Coachhouse Foods and Equipment Ltd
711 Lisburn Road
Belfast BT9 7GU
☎ 0232 381580/381570

sauter appliances

F. E. Smith Electrical Ltd
3/5 Camden Place
Dublin 2
☎ Dublin 751702

scholtes appliances

F. E. Smith Electrical Ltd
3 Camden Place
Dublin 2
☎ Dublin 751702
(*Republic of Ireland*)

G. & O. Services
Kilwee Industrial Estate
Upper Dunmurry Lane
Belfast BT17 0HD
☎ 0232 301121
(*Northern Ireland*)

school stationery

Some of the very best value in Dublin in school stationery and arts-and-crafts supplies is to be found in **K. & M. Evans**, 5 Mary's Abbey, Dublin 7, ☎ Dublin 726855.

septic tanks

It has been suggested that at least 50 per cent of the septic tanks in this country function inadequately, are badly designed and are badly maintained. Professionals reckon that there are around 300,000 septic tanks in operation in Ireland, which means at least a million people using septic-tank systems. That can add up to a plethora of problems. And there are thousands of new septic tanks installed every year.

A badly functioning septic tank can overflow on the surface of your garden and can be a serious health hazard in areas frequented by children and dogs and cats. It can flow into ditches, rivers and streams and into local ground water. It can smell badly. It can even pollute the well water of the owners, or indeed pollute other people's wells. Many tanks are simply not big enough to cope with the material going into them. Few tanks are regularly checked or maintained, and you tend not to give much thought to septic tanks as long as they don't prove troublesome. Action is only taken when a problem arises. There are no provisions for any regular checking or inspection of septic tanks by authorities once they have been installed. Indeed, there are no regulations in Ireland governing the building of septic tanks – just recommendations.

Many tanks are not big enough to begin with. In northern Europe professionals believe that one person produces seventy litres of sludge in the tank per year. The more people you have in the house, the more sludge is produced. The most commonly installed septic tank is one with a capacity to cope with a four-person household; yet in many households there are considerably more than four people.

Modern detergents can be actively harmful in septic tanks. We hear a lot about phosphates, and there is no doubt that phosphates can be detrimental to ground-water systems, but there are other ingredients which can also be harmful. An expert on septic tanks once told me that the two ingredients in modern detergents which would worry him most are bleaches and disinfectants, 'particularly some of the new ones which contain hypochlorite and which are supposed to kill all known bugs. That's just what they do. A septic tank needs bugs in it to function properly. I worry about the phosphates because of their eventual effect on ground water as a pollutant; but I think the effect of the phosphates on the actual septic tank is not very significant.'

There are certain situations – and certain soil conditions – in which a septic tank is more likely to have problems. Many people who have had on-going difficulties with their septic tanks might well be interested in a system which was introduced to Ireland a few years ago. It's called the Biocycle treatment system, and the idea comes from Australia.

Frank Cavanagh is a civil engineer with MSI, a mechanical civil engineering firm of over twenty years standing. He went to Australia to study the Biocycle system and came back enthusiastic. The actual tank is some six feet (two metres) in diameter, but most of this lies below the surface of the ground. In a nicely landscaped garden, all you should see of the system is a round, dark-green plastic cap, about six-feet wide, and even this can be disguised with shrubs and flowers. The tank is divided into four principal chambers: the receiving chamber, the aeration chamber, the clarification chamber and the irrigation chamber.

The receiving chamber operates in much the same way as the traditional anaerobic septic tank. All the waste gets primary treatment in this chamber. Sludge, the ultimate by-product of waste, is accumulated in this chamber, which Biocycle says only needs emptying on average every nine years. The displaced and partially treated waste flows from the receiving chamber to the aeration chamber. Air is supplied by means of a compressor. From the aeration chamber, the effluent flows into the clarification chamber, and then to the pump or irrigation chamber where it is chlorinated.

The water which eventually emerges from the system looks as clear as tap water and is dispersed through fine jets on a pipeline to irrigate any part of the garden in which you want it. Obviously, in Australia where water can be scarce, conservation of water in this way is highly desirable. But we would hardly need to water our plants as often as they do; the pipe could easily be directed to a drain or a ditch. The good thing is that whatever is produced doesn't smell, seems clean, and the company says that all tests on the unit so far have never recorded any presence of faecal coliform organisms. Indeed, it is a system which can solve problems for many people, and which has made it possible to build houses in spaces and areas that could not have been considered before. There have actually been cases of planning authorities stipulating the installation of a Biocycle system as a condition for planning permission.

The electricity involved in the Biocycle system uses about the same as a fridge would in a week, says Frank Cavanagh, and there is a warning system wired back to the switchboard which tells you if anything goes wrong. Three maintenance visits in the first year are included in the initial cost. After that, it costs about £100 a year for twice-yearly maintenance visits.

The Biocycle system operates here as a joint Irish-Australian venture. Fully installed, the system costs around £3,500, somewhat more than a traditional tank, but many people may feel that a more efficient system is worth the extra money. If you want to inquire further about **Biocycle**, write to **Frank Cavanagh** at 107 Baldoyle Industrial Estate, Dublin 13, or telephone him at ☎ Dublin 391347/391425/391000.

Septic tanks and detergents:

Ecover make a wide range of environmentally friendly products, and while many companies claim to be 'green', Ecover would seem to be more passionate and more committed than most. Their washing powders contain no petroleum-based detergents – petrochemical surfactants derived from mineral or petroleum oil are used in almost all kinds of cleaning products and are known under the common name of detergents. Ecover uses no phosphates, no optical bleaches, no chlorine bleaches, no enzymes and no synthetic perfumes or colourings. I can honestly say that since we started using Ecover in my own house some years ago, our septic tank has given us little or no trouble – and having lived with a septic tank for over twenty years I know the kind of trouble they can give. This has also been the experience of other septic tank owners with whom I've talked.

• servis appliances

Ideal Service
Kylemore Park West
Ballyfermot
Dublin 10
☎ Dublin 6266720
(Republic of Ireland)

Homecare Appliance Service
Abbey Trading Estate
Longwood Road
Newtownabbey
Belfast BT36 7LD
☎ 0232 365487
(Northern Ireland)

sewing

Needlecraft, 27 Dawson Street, Dublin, ☎ Dublin 772493, was started by Noel Flavin's parents in 1938. Today Noel runs it with his wife, Breed. They stock a huge range of sewing and craft materials – from patterns and kits, to an enormous selection of wools, threads and needles, including special craft equipment of all kinds. They are also generous with advice. Noel himself can knit and embroider, but he likes doing tapestries best of all.

Esperanza O'Callaghan of **Tir na nOg**, Academy Street, Cork, ☎ 021 272773, first came to Ireland from Spain thirty-five years ago. She brought with her superb skills as a needlewoman and designer, particularly of children's clothes, and has worked here for a number of big names. She opened Tir na nOg just a few years ago. She has a riotous selection of wools and embroidery threads, beautiful patchwork materials, hundreds of tapestry canvasses, thousands of buttons – the largest selection in the country, she says, from all over the world – soft furnishing trimmings, decorative motifs, lampshade frames, shoe bows and buckles, patchwork templates, quilling sets, and books on many crafts, from basketry to crochet work.

• sharp

Microwave ovens, music systems, TVs, video equipment and stereos:

Dimpco Ltd
Airport Road
Cloghran
Dublin 9
☎ Dublin 8428222

In Northern Ireland the Sharp range is serviced by Craigavon TV Service.

Craigavon TV Service
17 Logan Drive
Lurgan
Craigavon
Co. Armagh BT66 8DA
☎ 0762 326119/322505

Microwave ovens are serviced in Northern Ireland by Coachhouse Foods and Equipment.

Coachhouse Foods and Equipment Ltd
711 Lisburn Road
Belfast BT9 7GU
☎ 0232 381580

shavers

Gavins of Camden Street have been in the business of servicing and selling shavers for almost thirty years. If you have an old shaver to which you are devoted, but which needs a bit of attention, Gavins is the place to bring it. They keep a huge stock of spare parts. Most shaver manufacturers, like Philips or Remington, are prepared to supply parts for ten years, but not more. When the ten years on a particular shaver is up, Gavins buy all the remaining stocks of parts, which is why if you bring your twenty-year-old Philips or Remington along for repair, chances are they will be able to repair it for you.

Gavins also sell new shavers, mainly Braun, Remington, Philips and Payer. Since each of these manufacturers make a range of up to ten different shavers, you could see between thirty and forty models in Gavin's shop.

There are three different kinds of electric shavers: the foil-type shaver (most of the Remington shavers are this type), the rotary shaver (Philips shavers are all rotary), and a Remington shaver with the old solid-type head. Knowing which type of shaver to buy is not always easy. Ideally, the best way to find out is to use each shaver for a month or so and see how you get on with it. But this is hardly practical. As a general rule, it can be said that the foil-type shaver is not particularly suited to a very young or a very old beard. These kinds of beards are usually happier with the Philips rotary shaver. Shavers can also be powered in different ways. You can have a rechargeable shaver, a dry-cell battery shaver or a mains shaver. You can even get a shaver with gold-plated heads.

You may, of course, have a beard and not want an electric razor at all, but a beard trimmer. This is essentially a hairdressing unit – a bit like the old hairdressing cutter. Remington, Braun, Philips and Pifco do them, and some are more versatile than others. You may be a lady and want a lady's shaver. Gavins have them too, made by Clairol, Remington, Philips and Braun.

You'll find **Gavins** at 83 Lower Camden Street, Dublin, ☎ Dublin 757109. They're open every day from 9.00 a.m. to 6.00 p.m., six days a week. There are two Jims involved in the business, Jim Gavin and Jim Higgins, and they're both a good source of information.

In Northern Ireland contact the **Shaver Shop**.

The Shaver Shop
28 North Street Arcade
Belfast BT1 1PH
☎ 0232 231844

• shirts

The Kelso Laundry
Rathmines Road
Dublin 6
☎ Dublin 972089/978490

Kelso's offer a same day laundering service on weekdays.

The Laundry and Dry Cleaning Shops offer a twenty-four hour service. You'll find them at the following addresses.

The Laundry and Dry Cleaning Shops
118-120 Lower Rathmines Road
Dublin 6
☎ Dublin 962467

365 North Circular Road
Dublin 7
☎ Dublin 308558

23 Sandymount Green
Dublin 4
☎ Dublin 683962

The shops are open seven days a week, from 8.00 a.m. until 10.00 p.m. You can leave your shirts in on the way home from work and collect them the next evening.

• shoes (see feet and footwear)

showers

Showers are an essential part of any bathroom today. For many people, the shower is even more important than the bath, which gives the room its name. They find a shower more convenient, quicker and more refreshing, and there are those who will argue that a shower is also more hygienic.

Showers are also more economical on water, on heating costs, even on time. The amount of water that it takes to fill a bath can provide showers for two or three people; equally, the energy it costs to heat the water to fill one bath can heat the water for several showers. And two or three people can usually shower in the time it takes one person to soak in a bath.

There are, however, different types of showers, and it is worth doing a bit of research and exploration before you finally decide on the one you are going to install. In some showrooms you can actually see showers in action; this will give you a good idea of the strength of a particular appliance.

There is the very basic type of shower: the **bath/shower combination** installed over the bath. It consists of a hot/cold combination tap, hose and shower head. This is the cheapest form of shower, but it is generally unsatisfactory to use as you have to stoop to tap level to operate and control it, and if somebody turns on a tap elsewhere in the house, or flushes a toilet, the temperature of the shower can vary quickly.

If your shower is over the bath, special attention must be paid to the way the bath is cased into the surrounding wall. Obviously, good casing is important at any time, but in the case of a shower over the bath it's even more important because the danger of seepage is greater. If your bath isn't properly cased-in, you'll have seepage, which means water leaking down into the room below if your bathroom is upstairs, or damp under the floor if your bathroom is on ground-floor level. Good casing and impeccable tiling is the only answer.

There is the straightforward **combination shower in its own cubicle**. This draws hot and cold water from the hot-water cylinder and the cold-water tank respectively. This kind of shower is designed for easy temperature selection. The best type of combination shower has separate controls for spray force and temperature selection, which enables the user to select the perfect combination of spray and water temperature to suit. A distance of at least two feet (half a metre) is required between the handshower and the base of the cold-water tank.

There are two types of combination showers available. There is the mechanical mixer type, which requires equal hot- and cold-water pressure, and if the installation is not plumbed independently, the temperature can alter if water is drawn off elsewhere. Alternatively, there is the thermostatic combination shower, which overcomes this problem: the temperature selected will always remain constant. In addition, there is a maximum temperature stop which ensures temperature will never exceed the level chosen. This is ideal for use by children or elderly people.

Then there are the **instant electric showers** which run directly off the cold-water supply and heat the water instantaneously as the shower is turned on. The good thing about the instant shower is that it requires no hot-water storage, so that you can have a shower at any time, winter or summer, because you are not depending on an immersion group or central heating to heat your water. The bad thing is that the flow of water is not very strong. Where a combination shower is taking in water from two sources – the hot-water cylinder and the cold tank – the instant shower is taking it only from one source – the cold-water tank. So the flow is not going to be as good, particularly during the winter months when the cold-water supply is much colder anyway (because the water is colder, the flow rate slows down to enable the water to heat). On a very cold winter's day, the flow from an instant shower can be exasperatingly meagre.

There is a version of an instant shower with a built-in pump for connection to the cold-water tank, where cold-water mains pressure is inadequate. However, it should be noted that the pump here is only for operating the electric shower and does not provide a greater flow rate than the standard instant electric shower.

There is an excellent case to be made for an instant shower in a houseful of teenagers where somebody always seems to be showering or washing their hair at all hours. But if you are looking for a really powerful shower, the kind that is commonly seen in continental countries, which blasts the water at you with force and vigour, then the instant shower is not for you. You might like to consider a powered shower.

Recently, the demand for **powered showers** has increased dramatically. People with experience of powered showers in other countries, or in clubs or sports complexes here, often decide they would like to have one in their own home. The ultimate powered shower features two or four body-sprays on both sides of the cubicle, in addition to a flexible handset control.

Mira is one of the best-known names in showers, and **Modern Plant**, who import Mira showers, say that Mira is the only leading manufacturer who supplies all types of showers. Mira recently opened a new showroom at its premises on the Naas Road, a really excellent showroom where you can see up to twenty different kinds of showers working, including showers for the elderly and the handicapped or disabled: **Mira**, Otter House, Naas Road, Dublin 22, ☎ Dublin 591344.

The Mira showroom is special because a wide range of showers are shown, but there are also a number of other showrooms, hardware outlets and builders' providers, both in Dublin and around the country, where you can see showers in operation.

H 20 Pumps & Electrical Services – don't be misled by the name – are at Ballycorus, Kilternan, Co. Dublin, ☎ Dublin 2822025. They do very sophisticated, very powerful Hansgrohe showers, which are made in Germany.

Ideal Standard just recently opened a splendid new showroom at Erne Place, Holles Street, Dublin, ☎ Dublin 764445, with a first-class selection of bathroom ware and a variety of showers in operation.

You can also see working showers at the following addresses.

In Dublin:

Arcon Heating and Plumbing Ltd
6/7 Glenview Industrial Estate
Herberton Road
Dublin 12
☎ Dublin 541384

Bathroom World Ltd
45 Lower Kevin Street
Dublin 8
☎ Dublin 784614

Chadwicks Ltd
Dublin Industrial Estate
Glasnevin
Dublin 11
☎ Dublin 307811

Davies
6/8 Richmond Avenue
Fairview
Dublin 3
☎ Dublin 376076

Dublin Providers Ltd
68 Old Kilmainham
Dublin 8
☎ Dublin 531046

H. & V. Centre
North Road
Dublin 11
☎ Dublin 345457

P. H. Ross Ltd
16 Old Cabra Road
Dublin 7
☎ Dublin 385666

Smiths Building Supplies
Greenhills Road
Tallaght
Dublin 12
☎ Dublin 508056

Tubs and Tiles
1 Kylemore Road
Dublin 10
☎ Dublin 6264493/6264495

Outside Dublin:

Cork:

Cork Builders' Providers Ltd
Casey's Cross
Pouladuff Road
Cork
☎ 021 961700

Dublin Providers Ltd
Kinsale Road
Clarkesbridge
Cork
☎ 021 964955

Heating and Plumbing Centre Ltd
12 Cornmarket Street
Cork
☎ 021 277290

Hickey (Cork) Ltd
9-12 Maylor Street
Cork
☎ 021 273281

Irish International Trading Corporation
Rocksavage
Cork
☎ 021 275161

The Shower Shop
Rocksavage
Anglesea Street
Cork
☎ 021 962914

Tubs and Tiles
5 Penrose Quay
Cork
☎ 021 506944

Galway:

Morahan & Hughes Ltd
Tuam Road
Galway
☎ 091 51862

T. O'Higgins & Co. Ltd
Shantalla
Galway
☎ 091 22411

Kilkenny:

Tubs and Tiles
Industrial Estate
Hebron Road
Kilkenny
☎ 056 62244

Limerick:

Abbey Heating and Plumbing
Tipperary Road
Ballysimon
Co. Limerick
☎ 061 413722

Tubs and Tiles
Roxboro
Limerick
☎ 061 311206

Mayo:

Tony Scott Heating and Plumbing Supplies
Peter Street
Westport, Co. Mayo
☎ 098 25442

Sligo:

Tubs and Tiles
Castle Street
Sligo
☎ 071 70325

Tipperary:

Clonmel Plumbing Supplies
21 Upper Irishtown
Clonmel
Co. Tipperary
☎ 052 23422

Waterford:

Tubs and Tiles
Park Road
Waterford
☎ 051 77304

Westmeath:

Tubs and Tiles
Deerpark Road
Athlone
Co. Westmeath
☎ 0902 92755

In Northern Ireland **W. H. Leech & Son Ltd**, Unit 3, 34 Montgomery Road, Belfast BT6 9HL, ☎ 0232 401909, have just built a showroom for showers – very similar to that built by Modern Plant in Dublin – where you can see up to twenty different kinds of showers working, including showers for the elderly and disabled. But there are a number of other showrooms and plumbing outlets in Northern Ireland that are worth visiting and which show showers in operation.

Northern Ireland:

Bassetts Heating and Plumbing
Mahon Industrial Estate
Mahon Road
Portadown BT62 3EH
☎ 0762 339438

Beggs & Partners
Pennybridge Industrial Estate
Larne Road
Ballymena BT42 3HB
☎ 0266 45121

Central Merchants (Northern Ireland) Ltd
Nelson Trade Centre
Nelson Street
Belfast BT15 1BH
☎ 0232 329767

J. Frackleton & Son Ltd
25 Imperial Drive
Belfast BT6 8JH
☎ 0232 732231

Glenhill Merchants Ltd
Musgrave Park Industrial Estate
Stockman's Way
Belfast BT9 7ET
☎ 0232 669444

Haldane Fisher (North Down) Ltd
41a Bangor Road
Conlig
Newtownards BT23 3PX
☎ 0247 271711

Plumb Center
2-5 Whitla Street
Belfast BT15 1JP
☎ 0232 751626

Plumb Center
Lisburn Commercial Centre
Lisburn BT27 5EA
☎ 0846 602121

Shawmac Ltd
53-57 Batchelor's Walk
Lisburn BT28 1XN
☎ 0846 602216

T. A. Shillington & Son Ltd
Castle Street
Portadown BT62 1BD
☎ 0762 337321

Stevenson & Reid Ltd
8 Abbey Trading Estate
Longwood Road
Newtownabbey BT36 7PA
☎ 0232 852212

Stevenson & Reid Ltd
34 Cullybackey Road
Ballymena BT43 5DF
☎ 0266 49715

Stevenson & Reid Ltd
Ballybrakes Industrial Estate
Ballymoney BT53 6LQ
☎ 02656 65094

Paul Thompson Heating & Plumbing
35 Waringstown Road
Lurgan BT66 7HH
☎ 0762 881407

Shower repairs:

Stephen Perry of **Perrika Appliance Services**, The Lodge, 27 Willow Avenue, Greenpark, Dublin 22, ☎ Dublin 594709, specialises in repairing all types of showers.

• siemens appliances

Service:

Appliance Care
Unit 4, Ballymount Drive
Ballymount Industrial Estate
Walkinstown
Dublin 12
☎ Dublin 502655

Parts:

Charlie Shiels
Golden Bridge Industrial Estate
Inchicore
Dublin 8
☎ Dublin 545844
(*Republic of Ireland*)

Euro Serv (Ireland) Ltd
66 Dows Road
Drumbo
Belfast BT8 8LH
☎ 0232 826446
(*Northern Ireland*)

silver, repaired and replated

Sean Carroll & Sons Ltd
Granary Hall
18 Rutland Street
Cork
☎ 021 311757

Regal Silver
IDA Centre
The Coombe
Dublin 8
☎ Dublin 532646

William Egan & Sons of Cork had a prestigious reputation in the southern capital for over a century and a half. They were ecclesiastical outfitters: they made vestments, church furniture and church plates. They were also jewellers and silversmiths whose work was highly regarded countrywide. During the civil war in 1922, they even did their own hallmarking, rather than risk shipping pieces to the Assay Office in Dublin. These pieces are now known as republican silver and are very highly prized.

Over the years many fine craftsmen worked for Egans, and quite a few of them are now running businesses of their own in Cork. One of these craftsmen is **Sean Carroll**, who joined Egans in 1954, worked for them for over thirty years and was the last silversmith to leave the firm in 1984.

Sean now has his workshop in Granary Hall, Cork. He is passionate about his craft, and a visit to his workshop and an hour in his company are memorable experiences. He didn't get any redundancy money when he left Egans; instead, he received the tools and the plant. Even the benches come from Egans, and some of the tools are probably as old as Egans is itself. Sean makes a complete range of silverware, from strawberry dishes, tea-sets and silver cutlery, to Chippendale salvers, condiment sets and drinks measures. He still does the church work in which Egans specialised – he makes chalices, ciboria, pyxes, Eucharistic ministerial bowls, tabernacles, cruet trays and altar spoons.

When Tip O'Neill was given the freedom of Cork, he was presented with a scroll in a casket, handcrafted by Sean Carroll. During the Cork 800 celebrations, Sean and his two sons made a model of the Sirius, the first ship to bring Irish whiskey from Cork to North America, which was later presented to the city of Cork by Irish distillers. It took over two months to complete, and now stands in the Lord Mayor's office. He has made a sauce-boat and a strawberry dish for Pope John Paul II and more recently a copy of the Cork mayoral chain – the original, in solid gold, was deemed too precious to use on all but high ceremonial occasions. The copy was made in bronze and silver with a fine 24-carat-gold finish.

As well as crafting original silver pieces, Sean does some reproduction work, 'of styles rather than of particular items'. He also repairs gold and silver. If you have a piece which needs attention, he'll be happy to repair it or replate it for you. If you want to learn something about the craft, Sean can also help you – he teaches adult education classes in the Cork School of Art. What I found particularly fascinating was his own work bench. He has twenty-seven personal hammers. Every silversmith, he says, will have his own, but some of the ones he uses come from Egans and are well over a hundred-years-old. Lined up, in tidy rows, can be seen a cow-horn hammer, which is a traditional hammer for forming or 'raising' silver (the head is made from actual cow's horn, which has to be replaced every two to three months); metal hammers for 'raising' silver, though Sean says the cow-horn is better: 'Metal hammers are much more inclined to mark the silver, and then you have to get the marks out. A cow-horn hammer will crinkle rather than mark.'; a planishing hammer, which is used to smooth out the wrinkles; a rawhide mallet, used for tapping out and smoothing major creases and wrinkles; and much else besides.

There are, for example, special tools for special pieces. Included is a 'stake' for making a chalice cup or ciborium bowl, or for shaping a candlestick. There are levelling stakes for levelling trays. And there is also some machinery, although the bulk of the work is done by hand. As well, under each silversmith's bench is a cowhide bag, which hangs just below the immediate work area. This catches any filings or stray pieces of metal.

If you should happen to be in Cork, you can see a display of Sean's work in his own showroom in Granary Hall, Rutland Street, but you can also see his work in the tax-free shop at Cork Airport.

Regal Silver in the IDA Centre, Dublin, makes silver-plate holloware – trays, tankards, goblets, slavers and cups, including a lot of solid-silver pieces. As well as crafting pieces, they also specialise in repairing and replating old silver. Unless a piece is badly damaged and corroded, it is probably worth replating. In most Irish homes, for example, you will find some pieces of silver plate, perhaps a tea-set which has been handed down from mother to daughter. Even the best-plated tea-set will look the worse for wear after thirty or forty years. It is certainly likely to be tarnished, and the plate can also have worn away if it has been polished many times.

The base metal in a tea-set may be nickle, brass, pewter or copper. How well it wears – old or new – depends on how well it has been plated. Pat Carroll from Regal Silver told me that there was quite a flood of Indian silver on the Irish market recently which had only been 'flash plated' – that is, given a very thin layer of silver, which usually wore away after it was polished a few times. If you're buying a piece of silver plate, you should always ask how long the life of the plate is: is it ten, fifteen or twenty years? The thicker the plating, the longer it will last, and the more it will cost you. The manufacturer's stamp should also be a good indication of quality; at the very least, if the quality doesn't prove to be as good as you expected, you can take it up with the person who made it.

As I mentioned before, unless a piece is very badly damaged and corroded, it is worth replating. You can expect to pay between £70 and £90 to have a four-piece tea-set replated, and probably around £35 for an individual teapot. When you consider that a good silver-plated tea-set would cost you around £350 new, replating an old set can be money well spent. In Regal Silver's showrooms you can see a range of the pieces produced. They stock a large selection of individual silver-plated pieces and make solid-silver pieces to order. Quite a number of the trophies given in racing events, snooker and golf championships have originated from Regal Silver in the Coombe, as well as all the silver plating for A. T. Cross: the barrels, the caps and the clips on the Cross pens. Regal Silver has a range of pieces for corporate promotions – the kind of pieces which are given to clients as a gift – or to mark a special occasion – hand-mounted trays, plates, vegetable dishes, sauce bowls, hors d'oeuvre dishes, fruit bowls and butter dishes. Their showrooms are open every weekday from 8.00 a.m. to 5.00 p.m., including lunch-time. You will also see pieces of their holloware in leading stores around the country.

To find **Regal Silver** and the IDA centre in the Coombe, turn right at the main traffic lights after St Patrick's Cathedral as you come out of town. Go up Dean Street, turn left into Ardee Street and go straight across into Newmarket. The IDA centre is on the left-hand side.

• sirocco washers and dryers

Appliance Network Services Ltd
19 East Essex Street
Dublin 2
☎ Dublin 6795244/715528

• sleeping beauty electric blankets

Beaumark Service Company
Sunbury Industrial Estate
Walkinstown
Dublin 12
☎ Dublin 504620

• snowcap appliances

Ideal Service
Kylemore Park West
Ballyfermot
Dublin 10
☎ Dublin 6266720

• soda stream appliances

Kisch International Ltd
Unit G 1, Ballymount Drive
Ballymount Road
Walkinstown
Dublin 12
☎ Dublin 521411

Kisch also look after servicing in Northern Ireland.

• sony tvs, videos and cds

Sony Ireland Ltd
81 Broomhill Road
Tallaght
Dublin 24
☎ Dublin 519311
(*Republic of Ireland*)

Sony Ireland will be able to give you the name of your nearest service agent.

Belfast Sony Centre
7-9 Lower Garfield Street
Belfast BT1 1FP
☎ 0232 236983
(*Northern Ireland*)

• stained glass

Irish Stained Glass Ltd, Hanover Quay, Dublin 2, ☎ Dublin 773354/775878, was founded in 1957 by the father of the present owner, Alan Tomlin. They specialise in the repair and restoration of all stained glass: leaded panels, fire screens, lanterns, anything, in fact, which involves stained glass. They have a big collection of old Victorian acid-etched patterns, and Alan Tomlin says he is constantly adding to the collection: 'I come across a different old pattern almost every month.' They also make *new* stained-glass pieces. In recent years they have made sets of windows for churches in Banff and Vancouver in Canada, for churches in San Francisco, Palm Springs and San Diego in the US, and for churches in the UK.

Abbey Stained Glass Studios (IPCRA)
18 Old Kilmainham
Dublin 8
☎ Dublin 777285

John Devitt (IPCRA)
12 Avondale Road
Killiney
Co. Dublin
☎ Dublin 2853954

Michael Judd Studio (IPCRA)
Unit 53, IDA Centre
Pearse Street
Dublin 2
☎ Dublin 775655

• stanley cookers

If you are looking for parts or advice for your Stanley cooker and you live in the Dublin area, the best person to talk to is **Peter Clifford** of **Clifford Fireplaces**, Gardiner Lane, Dublin 1, Dublin 746457. If you live outside Dublin, contact **Waterford Foundry Ltd**, Bilberry, Waterford, ☎ 051 75911, for the name of your local dealer.

stencilling

Stencilling is a very ancient technique. It has been used for centuries to create repeat patterns of many kinds, in many different ways: exquisite Chinese silks, religious illustrations in Siam and Persia, and intricate geometric designs in India. Stencilling was used in Buddhist paintings, in European textiles, in tiles and manuscripts of the Middle Ages, in the beautiful work of the New England settlers, in early American commercially produced furniture, not to mention in the work of the arts-and-crafts movement, and in Art Deco and Art Nouveau. It is an art form which has been enjoying a particular popularity in recent years, and which most people can practice.

You can, for example, paint old furniture and stencil on a design in different colours. You can stencil a border or a frieze on your walls, around a window or on a mirror. You can stencil a design on a wooden floor or on fabrics. Indeed, any painted surface, except a glossy or shiny one, such as those on ceramics and glass, can be stencilled.

Not everyone is able to make the kind of stencils they would like. Pre-cut stencils have been available in Europe and in America for some time, designed by professionals, cut and ready to use. They are ideal for beginners or non-professionals. Now pre-cut stencils are available here.

Stencil-Line is an Irish company which designs and supplies original stencils, making it simple for anyone wishing to use stencilling in the home. If you don't want to do it yourself, but are keen on stencilling, they provide a complete specialist service, which gives you the chance to have any stencil projects carried out for you by experienced stencil artists. If you want a stencil exclusively designed for you, they can do that too. As well, if you want a special painting job done – ragwork, sponging, fantasy painting effects – a team will come to your house or place of business, if you live within a reasonable radius of Dublin.

For further information you can write to **Eileen Leahy** at **Stencil-Line**, Hamptown Studios, 1 Pinewood Green Hill, Hampton, Balbriggan, Co. Dublin, or telephone her at ☎ Dublin 413201.

• stone, conserved and restored

John Kelly (IPCRA)
Lithan
5b ASBC Jubilee Road
Newtownards BT23 4YH
☎ 0232 701479

• stoves

Joe Manifold
Glorney Chimneys
40 Sundrive Road
Kimmage
Dublin 12
☎ Dublin 967355

Joe is one of the nicest men you could meet in the heating field and one of the most knowledgeable. He has a good selection of stoves in his Kimmage showroom, and if you want advice of any kind about your heating, or if you have a problem chimney, Joe will be delighted to advise.

Dunwoody and Dobson, 32 Lombard Street East, Dublin 2, ☎ Dublin 772463, sell and service the well-known Jotul cast-iron Norwegian stoves; they also supply Morso cast-iron stoves and Yoeman stoves.

• stringed instruments

William D. Patterson
(IPCRA)
Mellifonts Town
Bartlemy
Co. Cork
☎ 025 36549

Hugo Vegter (IPCRA)
Ivy Cottage
Glenmore
Cobh
Co. Cork
☎ 021 813352

• sunbeam

Shavers:

Gavins Shaver Centre
83 Lower Camden Street
Dublin 2
☎ Dublin 757109

Gas barbecues:

Noel McCabe Distributors
Bluebell Industrial Estate
Dublin 12
☎ Dublin 502926

• swan appliances

The Spare Parts Centre, 9 North Frederick Street, Dublin 1, ☎ Dublin 726565, is a collection depot for Swan and Krups appliances in Dublin.

Or send appliances directly to **Krups Sales and Service**, Roxoboro Road, Limerick, ☎ 061 417844.

For service in Northern Ireland the best thing to do is to contact Moulinex/Swan Holdings for the name of your nearest service agent.

Moulinex/Swan Holdings Ltd
Moulinex Swan House
Albion Street
Birmingham B1 3DL
☎ 021 2001313/2001212.

swimming gear

White Leather Industries in Waterford are essentially a manufacturer of leather garments. Since May 1989, however, they have been making swimming aids for young children. The aids are intended for children from four months to seven years. They are made from nylon lycra and have built-in floats, which are part polystyrene. They come in two styles – a swimming band and a swimming suit.

David White, the managing director of **White Leather Industries**, Unit 6, Enterprise Centre, High Street, Waterford, ☎ 051 70688, says they have sold them into sports shops in towns all over Ireland and have found, to their surprise, that the gear is particularly suitable for handicapped children.

• tappan waste disposal

Electroservice
Long Mile Road
Dublin 12
☎ Dublin 518666

• technisonic tvs and videos

FMS
3 Arran Quay
Dublin
☎ Dublin 710055

• tefal appliances

Kisch International Ltd
Unit G 1
Ballymount Drive
Ballymount Road
Walkinstown
Dublin 12
☎ Dublin 521411

Tefal has a number of service agents throughout Northern Ireland.

Domestic Sales and Repair Services Ltd
219 Kingsway
Dunmurry
Belfast BT17 9SB
☎ 0232 301533

V. Leonard & Co. Ltd
44a Alliance Avenue
Belfast BT14 7LX
☎ 0232 745303/749326
(for the names of other agents in Northern Ireland)

Alternatively, you could ring Tefal Customer Services in the UK: ☎ 0604 762726.

• telefunken appliances

Consumer Electronics
Unit 16, Western Parkway
Business Centre
Lower Ballymount Road
Dublin 12
☎ Dublin 500144
(*Republic of Ireland*)

Tele Video Services
6 Kilwee Industrial Estate
Dunmurry BT17 0HQ
☎ 0232 617222
(*Northern Ireland*)

tent repair

If you have a tent or a trailer tent in need of repair, you might like to know that **O'Mearas**, the camping people, have a full-time seamstress who will carry out all repairs to canvas and trailer tents. If you have a broken zip, it can be repaired; if your tent frame is damaged, O'Mearas will look after you. If you are looking for a tent part or accessory, O'Mearas say that after over thirty years in the business, chances are they will have what you need.

You can call into **O'Meara Camping** at Ossory Business Centre, 26 Ossory Road, North Strand, Dublin 3, ☎ Dublin 363233.

• terim ovens and hobs

Robert Johnston
377b Antrim Road
Newtownabbey BT36 8EB
☎ 0232 342558

• texas appliances

Ideal Service
Kylemore Park West
Ballyfermot
Dublin 10
☎ Dublin 6266720

In Northern Ireland, Texas appliances are serviced by Ideal Service in Dublin.

• textiles, repaired and restored

Cathy McClintock (IPCRA)
Unit 18, 204 Kilroot Park
Larne Road
Carrickfergus, Co. Antrim
☎ 09603 51429

• thatchers

Thatching is a skill which has been passed down from one generation to the next in the Brereton family. If you want a new thatched roof made or an old one repaired, get in touch with **Christy Brereton, Moods,** Robertstown, Co. Kildare, ☎ 045 60303.

• thomson

TVs and videos:

Consumer Electronics
Unit 16, Western Parkway
Business Centre
Lower Ballymount Road
Dublin 12
☎ Dublin 500144
(Republic of Ireland)

Tele Video Services
6 Kilwee Industrial Estate
Dunmurry BT17 0HQ
☎ 0232 617222
(Northern Ireland)

Dishwashers:

Ideal Service
Kylemore Park West
Ballyfermot
Dublin 10
☎ Dublin 6266720

Parts:

Charlie Shiels
Golden Bridge Industrial Estate
Inchicore
Dublin 8
☎ Dublin 545844

• thor by thor (not those distributed by jackson) appliances

Appliance Network Services Ltd
19 East Essex Street
Dublin 2
☎ Dublin 6795244/715528

In Northern Ireland contact Teska Ltd for Thor by Thor appliances.

Teska Ltd
16 Cedarhurst Road
Newtownbreda
Belfast BT8 4RH
☎ 0232 644821

tiles

Jim McNaughton set up **Tilestyle** in Walkinstown, Dublin, in the late 1970s. **Tilestyle** moved from Walkinstown in 1990 to bigger and better showrooms at 89 North Wall Quay, Dublin 1, beside the Point Depot in Dublin's Dockland, ☎ Dublin 742900. The new showroom was a derelict shed when Jim took it over. 'It used to be an oil depot. Before that it was a salt store, and it's still known as the Salt Store. When we took it over, it was in very bad condition. The roof was holed and there was so much water on the floor that I have a photograph of myself rowing across it on a raft. The water was coming up from the Liffey and down from God.'

They put in a new floor and a new roof, but retained the old timbers and painted them white. A new skin was placed on the outside and insulation and glazing on top. They cut openings through the front walls and installed tall, airy windows. Professional gardeners added greenery to the background in the form of shrubs and plants. The whole effect now is of brightness and light. It's an ideal ambience in which to show off tiles. And Jim has a huge selection of tiles to show off: in stock, about twenty million, he reckons, and in the showrooms an impressive and varied display.

Tilestyle has an enormous range of tiles for all kinds of areas, including some very special ones. There are tiles from Italy, Mexico, the United States, Uruguay and Germany. From southern Italy, Jim has unique inlaid marble tiles – tiny pieces of marble arranged in elegant colourful designs. He also has genuine old tiles from all over Europe – from old chateaux and churches – as well as inlaid encaustic tiles from Africa, again mainly from ruined churches.

Tilestyle, beside the Point Depot, is open seven days a week.

Regan Tile Design
2 Corrig Avenue
Dun Laoghaire
Co. Dublin
☎ Dublin 2800921

Isabel Moore is from Scotland, Robin Moore is from England, and the Regan tile business originated in Belfast, where it was started by Isabel's sister, Margaret Regan. They do slate tiles from Africa, India and China. The colours are what immediately charm the eye – opulent, highly individual and natural colours. These are large tiles, rich with the colours of ages, and no two tiles are exactly the same. There are also handmade terracotta tiles from France and Portugal, each piece individually distressed to produce the eroded surface effect of a 200- to 300-year-old tile. Some tiles combine light and dark clays in an appealing swirling finish. You can see a selection of them, all laid down, on the floor of the Regan Studio Showroom at Corrig Avenue in Dun Laoghaire. Look out for the sign on the railings of the first house on your right as you go up from town.

There are four branches of Regan Tile Design in Northern Ireland.

Regan Tile Design
60 Bedford Street
Belfast BT2 7FH
☎ 0232 232009

56 Glenshane Road
Magherafelt
Co. Derry BT45 8RE
☎ 0648 43163

11 Clarendon Street
Londonderry
Co. Derry BT48 7EP
☎ 0504 360502

3 Downshire Road
Newry BT34 1DX
☎ 0693 66422

The Tile Works
Laura O'Hagan and Orla Kaminska
39 Avenue Road
South Circular Road
Dublin 8
☎ Dublin 535837

Laura and Orla both received a diploma in craft design from the NCAD, where they specialised in ceramics. Orla was a year behind Laura; they got together after college when they happened to meet and discovered that they were interested in the same kind of work.

Generally, when people consider purchasing tiles they tend to buy at big tile stores. The idea of buying hand-decorated tiles will seem attractive, but most people assume that such tiles are too expensive for the ordinary pocket. This isn't necessarily true. To begin with, as Laura pointed out, 'you wouldn't want hand-decorated tiles over all your walls. Most people just want a section or a panel. One hand-decorated tile would cost you between £10 and £15, and in a panel you might have ten or fifteen tiles – which would cost between £100 to £150.'

The Tile Works has made tiles for family kitchens, for Victorian fireplaces, for the Educational Building Society in Baggot Street, Dublin, and for Madigan's pub on North Earl Street, Dublin – there are two tiled Joycean scenes in the mens toilets. You can see their tiles in O'Brien's Sandwich Bar in Mary Street, in the Stephen's Green Centre and in Powerscourt. You can also view their work in Tuite and Sheridan, a butcher's shop in Mullingar; they won an award for this particular project.

Laura and Orla have built up quite a collection of their work, so you can go in and choose the kind of tiles you most like. Alternatively, you can bring them your own ideas and work out the design together.

If you would like to meet Laura and Orla, you'll find them at their Dublin address. After you turn into the South Circular Road, coming from the Camden Street direction, watch out for a large church on the corner of Bloomfield Avenue on your left. Turn into Bloomfield Avenue, take a sharp left down a lane, and follow the lane around the corner. The Tile Works is on your right.

toastess skillets

Beaumark Service Company
Sunbury Industrial Estate
Walkinstown
Dublin 12
☎ Dublin 504620
(*Republic of Ireland*)

Teska Ltd
16 Cedarhurst Road
Newtownbreda
Belfast BT8 4RH
☎ 0232 644821
(*Northern Ireland*)

toshiba

Audio equipment:

Nokia Smurfit
Unit 31, Western Parkway
Business Centre
Lower Ballymount Road
Dublin 12
☎ Dublin 568333

TVs, videos and audio equipment:

Decco Ltd
6 Prince Regent Road
Castlereagh
Belfast BT5 6RQ
☎ 0232 798444

Microwaves:

Smurfit Packaging Systems
Ballymount Road
Walkinstown
Dublin 12
☎ Dublin 507266
(*Republic of Ireland*)

Robert Johnston
377b Antrim Road
Newtownabbey BT36 8EB
☎ 0232 342558
(*Northern Ireland*)

tower appliances

Beaumark Service Company
2a Sunbury Industrial Estate
Walkinstown
Dublin 12
☎ Dublin 504620

In Northern Ireland contact the following distributors.

Teska Ltd
16 Cedarhurst Road
Newtownbreda
Belfast BT8 4RH
☎ 0232 644821

Domestic Sales and Repair Services
219 Kingsway
Dunmurry
Belfast BT17 9SB
☎ 0232 301533

• tricity appliances

Service:

Electroservice
Long Mile Road
Dublin 12
☎ Dublin 518666

Parts:

Charlie Shiels
Golden Bridge Industrial Estate
Inchichore
Dublin 8
☎ Dublin 545844
(*Republic of Ireland*)

Electrolux Tricity Bendix Service
Unit 3, Edenderry Industrial Estate
326 Crumlin Road
Belfast BT14 7EE
☎ 0232 746591
(*Northern Ireland*)

• triton showers

Earthridge International
Maynooth
Co. Kildare
☎ Dublin 628671l
(*Republic of Ireland*)

Domestic Sales and Repair Services
219 Kingsway
Dunmurry
Belfast BT17 9SB
☎ 0232 301533
(*Northern Ireland*)

typewriters

This is the age of the electric typewriter and the word-processer, but in many places around the country there are people who still use an ordinary manual typewriter. Some may even use a really ancient manual typewriter, and when I say ancient I'm talking about antique typewriters – typewriters which may be thirty- or forty- or fifty-years-old. I know a man who enjoys mending these kinds of typewriters. If you have one and it needs repair, you should get in touch with **Bob Blake** at 7 O'Brien Road, Walkinstown, Dublin, ☎ Dublin 521065.

uilleann pipes, repaired and restored

Eugene Lambe
Fanore
Co. Clare
☎ 065 76122

unidare heaters

Ideal Service
Kylemore Park West
Ballyfermot
Dublin 10
☎ Dublin 6266720
(*Republic of Ireland*)

Unidare Environmental Ltd
Unidare Works
Church Road
Seagoe, Portadown
Co. Armagh BT63 1UH
☎ 0762 333131
(*Northern Ireland*)

upholstery cleaning

Ideal Cleaning Services Ltd
Monkstown Farm
Dun Laoghaire
Co. Dublin
☎ Dublin 2801458

Advance Cleaners
Pinewood Business Park
Whitehall Road
Wexford
☎ 053 45500

Image Contracts
Knocknacally
Youghal
Co. Cork
☎ 024 92984

• vacuum cleaners

If you have a problem with your vacuum cleaner, you'll find the service agent listed alphabetically under the brand name.

• valor cookers

There is a big network of service agents around the country for cookers run on Calor Kosangas. Any dealer stockist will have a list. If you can't find one, contact **Calor Kosangas**, Long Mile Road, Dublin 12, ☎ Dublin 505000.

If your cooker is run on Flogas Ergas, contact **Flogas Ltd**, Dublin Road, Drogheda, Co. Louth, ☎ 041 31041.

If it is run on natural gas, contact your local gas company.

In Northern Ireland contact **Calor Gas (Northern Ireland) Ltd**, Airport Road West, Sydenham, Belfast BT3 9EE, ☎ 0232 458466, if your cooker is run on Calor Kosangas.

If it is run on Flogas Ergas, contact **Flogas (Northern Ireland) Ltd**, Airport Road West, Belfast BT3 9ED, ☎ 0232 732611.

• valve radios

Harry Winstanley worked in Cunningham's of Donnybrook in Dublin for forty-six years. He takes delight and pride in repairing old radios. Since Cunningham's closed, he is to be found in his new workshop at 12 O'Carolan Road, South Circular Road, Dublin 8, ☎ Dublin 534041.

• vax

Service and parts for the VAX machine:

Ideal Service
Kylemore Park West
Ballyfermot
Dublin 10
☎ Dublin 6266720

In Northern Ireland telephone ☎ 0800 838317 for the name of your nearest service agent. Or let **CareElectric** look after it for you by dropping into your local **ShopElectric**.

• viols, violas, violins, cellos and double basses, repaired and restored

William Hofmann Ltd
(William Hofmann and
Conchobhar Ruiseal)
Unit 1a, Greystones Shopping
Centre
Delgany Road
Greystones, Co. Wicklow
☎ Dublin 2873299

William D. Patterson
(IPCRA)
Mellifonts Town
Bartlemy
Co. Cork
☎ 025 36549

Hugo Vegter (IPCRA)
Ivy Cottage
Glenmore
Cobh
Co. Cork
☎ 021 813352

- **wallpaper, repaired and restored**

David Skinner (IPCRA)
Paper Conservation Studio
Celbridge Mill
Celbridge
Co. Kildare
☎ Dublin 6272913

washing and washing machines

Few homes today are without a washing machine. The idea of doing a big family wash with a scrubbing board and boiling pots of water would appal most housewives, and rightly so. A good washing machine is a very important piece of equipment in any house. When you go out to buy one, there are certain points which are worth remembering.

The temperature of the water, for example, is an important consideration in any wash, and many of today's clothes are made to be washed at lower temperatures – hand-hot or even cooler – so it's essential to have a machine which will be able to cope with all kinds of washes, from the very hot, to the cool, woollen wash. Go for a machine which offers you good temperature control, from the 30°C wash right up to the 90°C or 95°C wash. The temperature should be variable. The difference between a wash at 60°C and 90°C is quite considerable, so you should have the choice of using temperatures between the two. Most of the light clothes worn in summer should be washed at a really low temperature, like 30°C.

Always buy a washing machine with a filter which is easily accessible. In any family house, it's only natural that something will get caught in the machine at some time or other – buttons, a coin, earrings, a piece of Lego. In a machine with an accessible filter, you simply open it and take out whatever is caught. You do *not* want a machine which requires a serviceman to unstick it; rather, you want to be able to do the job yourself.

When you go to buy a machine, check the door catch. A good door catch is very important, and on the cheaper machines the door catch is not always good. Go for a machine with a stainless-steel drum. They wear better.

Check the after-sales service. Ask how much the call-out charge is and how much time it covers. Some charges are quite high, though a few distributors offer free parts and labour for a certain period of time; others just offer parts. As well, you may find that you can't go and collect the parts yourself, but have to call in the company's engineer; this labour can work out to be quite expensive. Check out the special service companies offer for both parts and labour – some are better than others.

Think about spin speeds. You will see machines with 800 speed spins, but some of these spins are more efficient than others. This depends to a great extent on the number of holes in the drum. Some machines have more holes than others, and the more holes there are, the more water will be extracted. This means that machines with the same spin speed will differ in the amount of water they extract. It's also worth looking for a machine which does low spin speeds as well as high ones. Certain garments, such as delicate fabrics, will benefit from a low spin speed. You also want a rinse hold, or spin-delay facility, so that your clothes aren't lying there well spun and well wrinkled because you are not there to take them out of the machine when they are finished.

Repairs:

If you have a problem with your washing machine, you'll find the service agent listed alphabetically under the washing machine's brand name.

watches

It can be difficult to get old watches repaired, especially the old type of gentleman's pocket watch. Replacement parts are hard to obtain. **McDowells** at 3 Upper O'Connell Street, Dublin, ☎ Dublin 744961/743184, may find that they cannot repair an old ladies wrist watch but that they can fit replacement movements.

Ken Homan is a man who takes pride in repairing old watches. Occasionally he can get replacement parts – there is a company in the United States which specialises in parts for old Walton and Elgin watches and for watches made by the

Illinois Watch Company. Sometimes Ken makes the parts himself, but since this can be a slow and painstaking process, it costs more money than an ordinary repair. Customers do not always appreciate exactly *how* much time and skill is involved. However, if you have a watch which you want repaired and you are prepared to pay for it even if it necessitates the making of special parts, then **Ken Homan** is the man who can probably do it for you. You can find him at 91 Sorrento Road, Dalkey, Co. Dublin, ☎ Dublin 2858364.

water

The Geological Survey office has an excellent little booklet on the subject of finding water. It's called *Water Wells: A Guide To the Development of Groundwater for Small Residential and Farm Supplies*. It gives, as briefly as possible, basic information about ground water in Ireland, together with sound, practical advice on obtaining a supply.

Armed with the guide and common sense, the Survey Office believes that a practical-minded farmer or householder should in most cases be able to choose a site for his well and see it through to a successful conclusion. Part one of the guide contains general information on what ground water is, where it is found and how it behaves. Part two is a step-by-step outline of how to set about getting a supply of ground water for your house or farm. It tells you how to estimate the amount of water you need, helps you decide where to sink the well, whether to have a dug well or a borehole, and how deep to drill and what yield to expect. There are detailed sections on the different methods of well construction, on pumps and pumphouses and on the kinds of problems that arise with wells.

If you want a copy of the booklet on water wells, you can get it by sending £2 to the **Geological Survey Office**, Beggars' Bush, Dublin 4, ☎ Dublin 609511.

• watercolours, repaired and restored

Susan Corr (IPCRA)
Paper Conservation Studio
48 Woodley Park
Dundrum
Dublin
☎ Dublin 2987661

Pat McBride (IPCRA)
Paper Conservation Studio
IDA Tower Complex
Pearse Street
Dublin 2
☎ Dublin 775655

David Skinner (IPCRA)
Paper Conservation Studio
Celbridge Mill
Celbridge
Co. Kildare
☎ Dublin 6272913

windows

Over the past twenty years double glazing has become very big business and, indeed, has much to commend it. Double glazing makes a house warmer and more comfortable, it conserves heat, which costs so much to produce, it soundproofs a room – outside traffic noises dull into the distance – and it adds to the value of your house. Window replacements become necessary for a certain number of householders every year, and it still makes sense to replace them with double-glazed units. Once you have to replace your windows at all, you will find that the difference in cost between single glazing and double glazing is not so very great – while the difference in results is considerable.

If you find yourself having to replace your windows completely and are considering double glazing, you may wonder which double-glazed windows to get. You can have timber windows specially made to take double glazing, or you can have aluminium windows or UPVC windows. Certain houses will look better with one type of window than another. Some people will prefer the appearance of wood and the feel of it, and there is no doubt that good wooden windows can look very attractive indeed, and certainly more in keeping with older houses – aluminium or UPVC would not seem right on a Georgian house.

In the past **timber windows** have received some bad publicity. Very often bad windows are found in the speculative house market, where shortcuts have been taken and windows have been made from wet timber with no preservation treatment. If you decide to get timber windows, it is important to seek advice – either from an architect or a good joinery manufacturer. Make the right choice in the first place, and a good timber window will last your lifetime and probably longer – look at the timber window in old buildings which have stood the test of time. But it should be emphasised that timber windows *do* need care and maintenance. This means varnishing the wood once a year, or treating it with one of the good timber preservatives on a regular basis.

Most people who installed double-glazed windows in the early days installed **aluminium windows**. The quality of aluminium can vary considerably, and very often you got what you paid for. Some of the lowest quotations for aluminium double-glazed units came from operators who worked in a backyard or garage with the minimum of overheads. They were not above cutting corners. These were the operators who usually vanished when customers had problems later on. Aluminium is a cold material. It can actually conduct outside cold into your room. To prevent this happening, aluminium windows are usually fitted with what's called a thermal break. It's important that this operates effectively, that it totally separates the internal from the external structure, and that it minimises any risk of condensation. If this is the case, aluminium requires very little maintenance.

UPVC windows have come on the Irish market more recently. UPVC stands for unplasticised polyvinyl chloride; it's a very tough material indeed. You can get UPVC windows which look like white-painted wood or natural wood. UPVC is also very flexible. It will adapt to practically every shape or style, from bay windows to cottage to ultra modern. It can be made to exact and individual measurements and provides a natural barrier – unlike aluminium, it is not cold to the touch. UPVC doesn't burn, it has no porocity, which means no dirt can be ingrained into it, and it is now required in buildings where food is processed and where hygiene is essential. The surface is like glass and very hard; as you might expect, it needs only the minimum of maintenance. UPVC has been shown to perform well in widely varying weather conditions throughout the world.

Your ultimate choice of window will be personal, but whether you are buying wooden, aluminium or UPVC windows, you should check the credentials and experience of the installer carefully before you commit yourself to a purchase. Don't just choose the cheapest estimate. This is not necessarily the best; in fact, it could be the worst and the most expensive in the long run. Look for quality, expertise and a good track record.

Problems with sash windows:

People today are more and more aware of the necessity of conserving the beautiful things in our heritage. Those who buy old houses often take great pains to restore and refurbish them as faithfully as possible to their original state. Many of the loveliest old houses in Ireland go back to Georgian or Victorian times and have sliding sash windows made of timber. Some of these windows are more than a hundred-years-old. They were made with first-class timber, which had been properly dried, and were maintained by regular painting. The only problem is that they tend to rattle and let in draughts, or they jam and stick.

Anybody who has lived with sash windows that obstinately refuse to move, indeed, anybody who has been irritated by windows that rattle and let whining winds in on cold winter nights, will be familiar with the exasperation that makes you feel the only course is replacement. It isn't the only course. In 1983 a Yorkshire engineer called Robert Tunicliffe invented what is called the Ventrolla draught-proofing system specifically for these windows. His invention subsequently won him the United Kingdom Design Council Award in 1986. **W. & J. Bolger (Conservation) Ltd**, the well-known building contractors and joinery experts, are the franchisees for the system in Ireland. The Ventrolla system is installed in a window in about two hours and is subsequently invisible. There are no sheets of glass and no secondary frames. The window looks exactly the same as before, but is draught-proof and opens and closes easily.

'People who want to retain the character of a Georgian or Victorian house must retain the timber; but windows that won't work properly can be very irritating, and I can fully understand this irritation', says Billy Bolger of W. & J. Bolger. 'We're saying there is a solution, and we've got it in the Ventrolla system. It really does transform the performance of original sash windows and gives all the benefits of replacements, but at a fraction of the cost.'

You'll find **W. & J. Bolger (Conservation) Ltd** at Ardee Street, Dublin 8, ☎ Dublin 530377/530378.

In Cork the Ventrolla system is installed by **Tolkien (Conservation) Ltd**, The Mills, Blarney, Co. Cork, ☎ 021 381575.

And in Northern Ireland the system is installed by **T. & E. Lowry**, 1 Ardmore Avenue, Ormeau Road, Belfast BT7 3HD, ☎ 0232 646419.

Window draughts:

If you have windows or doors which let draughts in, you might like to consider the Curadraft system of draught-sealing. Draughts are not just a problem with old houses. Many modern houses, even those that are newly built, can have windows which allow the cold wind in. The Curadraft system is a relatively inexpensive but effective way of eliminating draughts. It can be used on casement windows, whether they are made from wood, metal, UPVC or steel. The materials used are discreet – you won't see them unless you go looking – and the cost is relatively low.

W. & J. Bolger (Conservation) Ltd at Ardee Street, Dublin 8, ☎ Dublin 530377/530378, install the Curadraft system.

Aluminium window and door repairs:

Simarc Engineering Co. Ltd
4a Kilbarrack Industrial Estate
Sutton
Dublin 5
☎ Dublin 393679

- **zanussi appliances**

Electroservice
Long Mile Road
Dublin 12
☎ Dublin 518666
(*Republic of Ireland*)

G. & O. Services
Kilwee Industrial Estate
Upper Dunmurry Lane
Belfast BT17 0HD
☎ 0232 301121
(*Northern Ireland*)

- **zaratov refrigerators**

Ideal Service
Kylemore Park West
Ballyfermot
Dublin 10
☎ Dublin 6266720

- **zerowatt appliances**

Robert Johnston
377b Antrim Road
Newtownabbey BT36 8EB
☎ 0232 342558